W9-BFZ-333

WINDOW
gardens

for windows, walls, decks, and balconies

JANE FORSTER
STEPHEN ROBERTS

FROM THE EDITORS OF COUNTRY LIVING GARDENER

HEARST BOOKS
NEW YORK

Library in Congress Cataloging-in-Publication Data

Roberts, Steve, 1948-
Window gardens : cameo designs for windows, walls and
balconies / Steve Roberts, Jane Forster, and the editors of
Country living gardener.
p. cm.
ISBN 1-58816-071-8
1. Window gardening. 2. Container gardening. I. Forster,
Jane, 1944- II. Country living gardener. III. Title
SB419 .R565 2002
635.9'678--dc21   2001039859

Conceived and produced by Breslich & Foss Ltd., London
Printed and bound in China
1 2 3 4 5 6 7 8 9 10

www.cl-gardener.com

contents

introduction

In *Window Gardens* Jane Forster and Stephen Roberts show you how to create beautiful displays for window sills, walls, decks, and balconies. The book demonstrates that you do not need a spacious garden in order to design eye-catching planting schemes. Each project uses an array of plants to suit different situations and tastes. In "Playing with Color," contrasting, balancing, or harmonizing colors are used to give different effects. The color of the surrounding walls and the container are also used as part of the overall design, creating some stunning effects. The chapter "Timeless Classics" features a multitude of classic plantings of window boxes and hanging baskets, plus some modern reinterpretations. Try planting salad vegetables for a tasty hanging basket, or harebells and lavender in a formal box for a wispy design that will ripple in the breeze.

If you are short on time or looking for a scheme to enhance a beautiful view, there are plenty of ideas in the "Pure and Simple" chapter. Plant strawberries and herbs to create a fabulous summer kitchen garden, or use single pots of chrysanthemum cultivars to frame a seaside view. Problematic places are given striking design solutions in "No Problem Places": even the windiest, hottest, or dampest areas can be given a splash of color with these ingenious planting schemes. The chapter "All You Need to Know" provides invaluable information on constructing and decorating your own containers, securing hanging baskets, plus tips on how to spot and eradicate plant pests and diseases. It also has helpful information on selecting and propagating plants, so novice and experienced gardener alike can get the most out of the planting schemes included in this book. The plant directory has further information on every plant used in the designs. This book contains all the information you need to get the most out of your window gardens, keeping them fresh, colorful, and interesting throughout the year. Happy planting!

playing with color

Why are so many gardeners afraid of color? Don't let unfortunate experiences with interior decorating put you off: paint is much more difficult to work with than flowers, and you will be amazed at how well unusual combinations can work in the garden. Nature not only is very forgiving but seems to want to help the gardener succeed.

Playing with color is not just about using strong colors but also about using more subtle palettes or even taking a minimalist approach and using black and white with soft green tones. Color can affect our mood: it can brighten a dark winter's day, bring a touch of hopeful light to spring mornings, or cool a hot summer scene. We hope that you will be inspired to try the planting schemes in this chapter.

purple boxes all in a row

The unusual shape of this window cried out for a visually strong display and one with an equally distinctive twist. Instead of one long box, a series of square boxes was used, each one large enough to take three or four plants. Not only does the repeating pattern of the boxes add extra interest, it also opens up the possibility of other configurations, such as fitting the boxes

around the corner of a balcony, and using them singly or in pairs on smaller window sills. Ingenious use of chicken wire and twigs adds unusual texture to the sides of the boxes. The creamy yellow wall behind the strong purple boxes becomes part of the complementary color scheme.

spring promise

Spring is the time when the garden explodes into a riot of fresh, bright colors, a moment captured beautifully in this vibrant display, which holds the promise of hot summer days to come. Don't be afraid to use strong hues: an extraordinary palette is at your disposal.

There are three main colors in this scheme: the deep purple of the boxes, the rich salmon red of the tulips and primulas, and the creamy yellow

of the polyanthus primroses and the wall. Part of the success of this scheme is due to purple and yellow being complementary colors (the other complementary color pairs are blue/orange and red/green).

CONTAINERS

The boxes were made from ½ in. (12mm) marine plywood, 6 in. (15cm) high and 10 in. (25cm) square. The wood was covered with a 1 in. (2.5cm) chicken wire mesh. Twigs were pushed between the box and the mesh and cut off at the top and bottom, level with the box. The whole box was then painted with a purple wood stain to create a strong, textured look.

PLANTS AND PLANTING

1 *Hyacinthus* 'City of Haarlem'
A beautiful, soft yellow hyacinth with good strong stems. This flower will add a beautiful fragrance to the spring display.

2 *Primula* Polyanthus hybrids The polyanthus is a type of primula that is derived from *P. vulgaris*, but it bears a cluster of flowers at the end of a sturdy, 4 to 6 in. (10 to 15cm) stem instead of having individual flowers on fine, wiry stems as the English primrose does. Polyanthus seeds are available from most spring and summer bedding and pot plant seed suppliers. Germinated seedlings and plugs are also easy to obtain, though flower color is only determined when buds appear. Established plants make a showy addition to any spring planting scheme. The polyanthus used here is in the traditional primrose yellow color.

3 *Primula vulgaris* These salmon-colored primroses have been selected out of mixed seedlings. Pot-plant type primroses are very popular, and as they are cheap to produce the growers have developed them in a wide range of colors, patterns, and sizes, so you can be sure to find one to suit your needs. This one forms a compact, bushy plant that reaches a height of between 2 ½ and 4 ¾ in. (6 to 12cm).

4 *Tulipa kaufmanniana* hybrids These short-stemmed tulips flower early. There is a wide range suitable for this type of planting, so make a selection based on your color scheme.

The spring boxes (left) have been arranged to take full advantage of the location. Their position on the steps emphasizes the different heights of the plants.

CARE AND MAINTENANCE

All the plants were brought on in individual plastic pots then planted up in a soilless potting mix in the boxes as they reached the flowering stage. As long as watering is sufficient and drainage good, the plants should thrive. Once flowering is over, the primroses and tulips can be planted out in the garden. It is best to lift the tulip bulbs once the leaves have died down. Dry out the bulbs before planting them back in the garden in the fall.

ALTERNATIVES

One of the great advantages of these boxes is that they can be used individually and not just in a row, which allows the possibility of a variety of arrangements. The spring flowers lend themselves to single-species planting, with separate plant types massed in each box. This style of planting in individual containers has a more modern, sculptured look than a mixed planting, focusing the attention on the texture and rich blocks of color of the plants.

fall purple

Fuchsia pink and deep purple plants accentuate the vibrant color of the boxes, with touches of green and white giving balance to the scheme. Leaves and berries bring much of the color to the planting, as well as adding a variety of textures.

PLANTS AND PLANTING

1 *Aster novi-belgii* (New York asters) Dwarf asters are used as an anchor plant for this design. Their yellow centers pick up the color of the wall.

2 *Brassica oleracea* This purple-centered ornamental cabbage gives a solid, round form to

any planting scheme. The color of the center intensifies as night temperatures drop.

3 *Erica* White heather peeking out from the back of the window box brings a touch of brightness and lightness to the color scheme. There are lots of good, hardy, white-flowered varieties of heather available.

4 *Cyclamen persicum* Miniature cyclamen add a particular vibrancy to this scheme, thanks to their strong, glowing color.

5 *Gaultheria mucronata* The pink berries of this plant, which is commonly called pernettya, add a change of texture and strengthen the color theme of the overall planting. There are several compact, pink-berried varieties of pernettya that would be suitable for this box.

6 *Hebe* 'Autumn Glory' This fall-flowering hebe was chosen for its rich purple flowers, which match the color of the boxes.

7 *Soleirolia soleirolii* (baby's tears) A good filler, this plant was used to tumble over the front of the box and soften the edges.

CARE AND MAINTENANCE

A standard soilless potting mix (readily available from garden centers and supermarkets) was used, with some slow-release fertilizer granules added before planting. The slow-release fertilizer should see the plants right through the growing season. However, care must be taken with the watering to make sure that every one of the boxes is watered properly.

ALTERNATIVES

Pot chrysanthemums, fall-flowering Universal Hybrid strain pansies, and fall-flowering heathers would be good alternatives for this design.

Another attractive alternative would be to create a scheme of single-species planting. Use *Colchicum* for a striking effect. This is a fall-flowering bulb with delicate blooms similar to those of a large crocus, that come in a range of colors from white through purplish pink. The flowers are carried on fragile white stems. The leaves come up in spring.

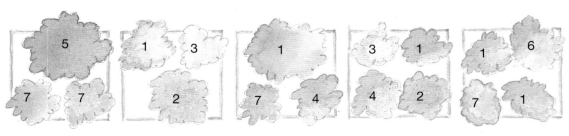

blue and white

Set against blue and white walls, these traditional wirework containers make a colorful spring picture, the delicate wirework echoing the fragile forms of the spring flowers. A freshness of color and simplicity of shape distinguishes these flowers, and planting them in small mixed groups set against the soft texture of moss creates a natural look.

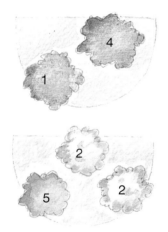

The location demonstrates the enhanced effect of a scheme in which plants, planters, and setting complement each other. Not only does the blue archway create a perfect background for the spring planting, it provides protection for the more delicate flowers, preventing them from being buffeted by wind and rain.

CONTAINERS

These traditional English wirework baskets were chosen for their delicate shape and classic style.

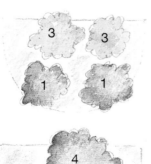

Moss was used to line the containers; use sheet or sphagnum moss, both of which are readily available from good garden centers. An inner plastic planter with drainage holes helps water retention.

PLANTS AND PLANTING

1 *Anemone blanda* The bright blue of this little woodland anemone is a true harbinger of spring. When the sun comes out and the flowers fully open they can be seen in all their beauty.

2 *Erythronium revolutum* An unusual and graceful spring bulb that thrives in well-drained soils and does best in partial shade. Its delicate form and subtle color complement the clear blues and yellows of the other flowers. An alternative to this is yellow-flowered 'Pagoda'.

3 *Iris danfordiae* This interesting species of iris, with a dwarf habit, grows to about 4 in. (10cm) high. The large, canary-yellow flowers are splashed with a beautiful olive green.

4 *Muscari armeniacum* The elegant spires of these deep blue grape hyacinths are particularly delicate and add height to the plantings.

5 *Primula* Wanda Hybrid strain This delicate creamy yellow primrose was selected from mixed seedlings of the Wanda strain.

CARE AND MAINTENANCE

As long as the bulbs are planted in a good quality, open-textured, soilless potting mix they will thrive. The anemones will bloom over a long period, giving excellent value for money. Deadhead the muscari after flowering. The woodland type of plants in this planting prefer a position in light or dappled shade.

tones of terracotta

The color and texture of this rough terracotta wall inspire a warm, exotic, Mediterranean look. The key to the planting's success is total simplicity. A line of bricks set diagonally across the wall beneath the tiny window give a strong structural element to the building, which is repeated by the line of terracotta pots. The scale of all three planting schemes—both pots and plants—was designed to be proportional to the window.

bowls of roses

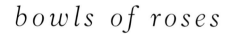

Red roses against terracotta create a wonderfully rich fall scheme that demonstrates how using tones of a single color can produce a strong design. This planting is in keeping with the simplicity of the scene, the use of only one plant type helping emphasize the pattern of bricks and planters. These miniature roses are available throughout the year. In the late summer and early fall they make a welcome addition as other plants are dying down or looking past their best.

CONTAINERS

Unfortunately, these irresistible terracotta plant holders are not frost proof, so in areas with freezing winters they are suitable for late spring, summer, and early fall schemes only. They are shaped with a flat back that allows them to hang safely on a wall and not blow around in the wind, while their bulbous shape has room for good root development.

PLANTS AND PLANTING

Use one or two miniature or patio roses for each pot depending on the size of the plants. With most roses, the flowers come in flushes, and these miniature varieties are no exception. If plants are bought in bud, the first flush will last for up to a month; deadheading will produce handsome dividends in the way of a very good, though smaller, second flush.

CARE AND MAINTENANCE

Unglazed terracotta is porous and will dry out rapidly in the sun, so careful monitoring of the pots is needed. Watering at least twice a week will be required throughout the season. In warm, sunny weather watering will be necessary every day, and possibly twice a day. As with all relatively small containers, regular feeding is important throughout the growing season. Use a balanced or high-potash liquid fertilizer.

ALTERNATIVES

Other plants that would provide reliable fall
color include outdoor pot chrysanthemums,
small pots of pernettyas in full berry (white-
or red-berried varieties would look good here),
or small autumn-flowering hebes.

hot summer

The colors and plants of the Greek Islands
combine (left) in a harmony of reds and oranges.
The pelargonium, so beloved in Mediterranean
countries, is used here but in a surprising way—
its foliage contributing as much to the color
scheme as its bright flowers.

PLANTS AND PLANTING

1 *Lantana camara* A lovely summer subject
for the window box and container garden.
Multicolored flowers appear in clusters, with
varying shades of orange, pink, and yellow
within the same cluster.

2 *Pelargonium* 'Vancouver Centennial'
The variegated leaves of this plant have a rich
bronze-terracotta center and a light green edge,
making a really striking combination. The bright
red-orange flowers are as dramatic as the
foliage, and the contrast between them creates a
truly eye-catching display.

CARE AND MAINTENANCE

A soilless potting mix is suitable for these plants. Neither plant is frost hardy, so both will need protection in areas with cold winters. If you are careful and purchase good-sized pelargoniums at the beginning of the season, you will be able to take and root at least one cutting from each plant and thus double your stock without depleting the planters.

spring purple

Playing with strong color combinations can be fun. Experiment with contrasting colors and different plant shapes for some dramatic effects. This spring planting of purple crocus against a terracotta wall (right) is a perfect example of using warm and cool colors to create contrast and bring a touch of brightness to dull spring days.

PLANTS AND PLANTING

Plant the corms about 3 in. (7.5cm) deep and the same apart. Crocuses are among the first harbingers of spring and are well worth growing in pots to bring indoors, too.

1 *Crocus* 'Remembrance' This is a very good variety that is readily available. It is rich purple with large shiny flowers. Using the plunging method of planting up the terracotta pots will extend the flowering period. Select plastic pots that fit inside the terracotta pots and plant the crocus in them, only plunging them into the display when they begin to bloom. As the flowers fade, the whole pot can be easily removed and replaced with a fresh pot containing just-blooming plants.

Alternatively, if you are going to plant directly into terracotta pots you should soak them first in a bucket of water, otherwise the dry, porous pots will draw moisture out of the potting mix. Air-dry them before use.

CARE AND MAINTENANCE

A general purpose, soilless potting mix is fine for crocus corms. The shelter and warmth of the house wall will encourage the flowers to open early, but the potting mix will dry out quickly in such a situation. Frequent watering will be necessary to keep the soil just moist at all times. Once the leaves have died down, the corms can be lifted and dried off, ready for replanting in the garden later in the year.

ALTERNATIVES

To follow on from the crocus, try some of the short-stemmed daffodils, such as 'Little witch' or 'Tête-à-tête'. Short-stemmed ornamental onions, such as *Allium oreophilum*, are ideal for color later in the season.

summer balcony

A profusion of color and texture cascade over the edge of this balcony—indeed, to be able to use plants in such liberal quantities is one of the great joys of planting summer displays. The variety of plants used contributes to the look of abundance, but by choosing pastel colors in close harmony as well as an appearance of unity a restful feeling is brought to the design. The mass of muted foliage creates a background for the brighter flower colors, framing them against the pale terracotta of the walls. The gray-green of the foliage reflects the color of the railings that encircle this elegant little balcony, helping to draw the whole scheme together.

The proportion of foliage to flower in this scheme is important, and adds to the feeling of abundance. An emphasis on a large volume of flowers can dominate the foliage and over-balance the design, whereas here the flowers nestle among the leaves to give a supremely natural appearance. Touches of lilac and mauve from the cool side of the spectrum extend the color range and help balance the hotter pinks of the pelargoniums. The leaves of the fuchsias add depth to the scheme, forming an ideal background for the tubular salmon-orange flowers. Fuchsias are excellent for container planting, and will extend the flowering period of this planting into late summer and early autumn.

CONTAINER

Because of the semicircular shape of this balcony, a container had to be constructed specially. First, a template was made in the shape of the balcony floor. The base and back of the trough were cut out of ½ in. (12mm) marine plywood and screwed together. The curved front was then measured and cut from flexible ⅛ in. (4mm) plywood and screwed to the base and back panel. The box was painted with plant-safe wood preservative, then lined with plastic to aid water retention in dry weather. Holes were punctured in the base of the lining to allow for drainage.

PLANTS AND PLANTING

1 *Artemisia absinthium* (wormwood) The silvery gray foliage of this aromatic plant is used at the back of the display to soften the profile and to link the scheme to the blue-gray railings.

2 *Fuchsia* 'Gartenmeister Bonstedt' This bush fuchsia has tubular flowers about ¾ in. (2cm) long in a salmon-orange color. It has rich green foliage and will flower throughout the summer. It is not frost hardy but will overwinter if protected, ready for use the following year.

3 *Helichrysum petiolare* This trailing plant is grown for its blue-gray foliage and is rewarding if well watered. The cultivar 'Limelight' used in this design adds the bright flash of lime green at the center of the balcony.

4 *Impatiens walleriana* The pink busy Lizzies used were chosen from the Tempo Hybrid strain, but a wide variety of reliable strains is now available. Most busy Lizzies act in the same way, giving lots of flowers throughout the summer. The plants grow to about 8 in. (20cm) in diameter and 4 to 6 in. (10 to 15cm) high.

5 *Laurentia axillaris* (isotoma) 'Blue Star' The blue flowers of this delicate plant reinforce the blue tones introduced by the scaevola. The feathery foliage adds a light texture to the center of the group.

6 *Pelargonium peltatum* 'Decora Rosa' A good, strong-growing pelargonium with a lax habit that gives the impression it is trailing. The warm salmon-pink flowers will be produced again and again throughout the summer.

7 *Pelargonium multiflora* type 'Atlanta Series' Two colors of this bold-flowered pelargonium

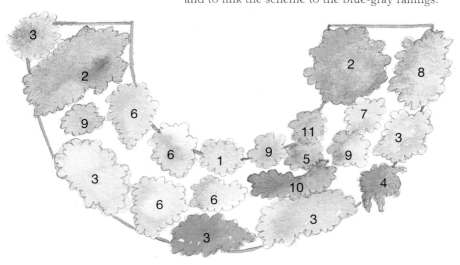

were used: a pale ice pink and a deep mid pink. These plants have a sturdy, bushy habit and give a solidity to the planting. They are good value, producing a large number of blooms per plant.

8 *Petunia* Surfinia hybrids   These hybrids flower in profusion over a very long period, especially if they are regularly dead-headed. New plants can be bought each year, but a plant that is overwintered in a frost-free place will provide plenty of cuttings that are easy to root in spring. The variety used in this box has two-tone violet flowers and variegated leaves.

9 *Petunia* 'Super Cascade' This is one of the original cascade type of petunias for hanging baskets. The flowers are weather tolerant and occur in a range of bright and pastel shades.

10 *Scaevola aemula* The blue flowers of this trailing plant mingle with the lime green and gray foliage of the helichrysums. They extend the colors into the cooler hues, while keeping to the soft tonal range of the other flowers.

11 *Verbena* There is a good choice of varieties of these popular trailing plants. Most are scented, but the paler flowers tend to have the stronger fragrance

CARE AND MAINTENANCE

The trough was filled with a general purpose, soilless potting mix, to which slow-release fertilizer with a high-potash content was added.

The evergreen stems of the helichrysum should be pinched back regularly to encourage fresh growth and to keep the plant bushy. The flowers produced are nondescript and should be removed as they appear. All the flowering plants, particularly the pelargoniums, should be deadheaded throughout the season and any straggly stems of verbena cut back. Give regular applications of high-potash liquid fertilizer through the growing season.

ALTERNATIVES

Plectranthus and nepeta would be excellent trailing plants for this summer design. The use of trailing Surfinia petunias or fuchsias can be extended to give a wider range of colors. For a more permanent planting, variegated ivy will give a trailing framework to which a range of spring bulbs or autumn chrysanthemums can be added to give color early or later on in the year, thus making the most of the balcony boxes.

Several of the plants used in this scheme are easily grown from softwood cuttings taken in early spring. Remove plants from the balcony before the first frosts and overwinter your stock plants in a frost-free conservatory or greenhouse. In late winter, increase the amount of water the plants are given and start to feed them so that they produce plenty of healthy young shoots to be taken as cuttings early in the spring.

black on black

If bright colors are not to your taste, experiment with subtle combinations or single-color planting schemes. These boxes demonstrate a very modern approach to design that makes use of stark color contrasts—black against warm white and green—combined with the strong geometric shapes of both boxes and plants. The result is a striking display that is perfect for a city balcony or window.

Successful plantings occur when all the elements of location, container, and plants work together, each bringing out the inherent qualities of the other. These boxes have been given a finish that blends with the black leaves of the ophiopogon and contrasts with the fleshy leaves of the echeveria, as well as echoing the striations of the slate wall. The soft pinkish pebbles act as a foil to the strong black shapes, and reflect the warm tones of the echeveria stems.

CONTAINERS

These boxes are made from ½ in. (12mm) marine plywood painted with a black ash-colored outdoor wood preservative. Once the stain dries, rub the boxes down with coarse sandpaper, working with the grain not across it. This removes the stain in places, exposing the texture of the wood and giving a weathered look. Drill four or five holes in the base of each box to ensure free drainage.

PLANTS AND PLANTING

The position of the different plants is critical with this style of box. In cold areas, plunge the potted echeverias into the soil mix pot and all, so they can easily be replaced with more frost-resistant plants when the weather turns cold.

1 *Echeveria* A range of echeverias is used in this grouping. These beautiful succulents have strong rosette shapes formed by concentric swirls of broad, fleshy, green, gray-green or blue-green foliage. They are not frost hardy and must be taken in during the colder months. Sempervivums (hen-and-chicks), which are frost hardy, could be used as a replacement.

2 *Ophiopogon planiscapus* 'Nigrescens' The black straplike leaf of this plant looks extremely good in containers that are intended for urban settings, and those that require a modern feel, or for natural settings where a contrast is required between texture, form, and color. This plant is hardy to zone 6.

seasonal color

This little cottage window set in a mustard-yellow wall stirs memories of hot days and Indian summers. The three schemes shown here are all inspired by the rich setting. The two summer plantings could not be more different: one is a riot of hot colors, the other a cool cascade of soft cream, silver, and pale purple. When the summer is over, our third scheme brings together some unusual color combinations in a splendid fall window box.

vibrant summer color

A simple cottage window is the perfect setting for this profusion of summer plants (right). The aim was to create an abundance of color against the mustard wall. This celebration of summer encompasses the whole spectrum from violet-blue *Monopsis* 'Midnight', through deep purple petunias, to red lobelia, and the soft yellow lily.

CONTAINER

Make a wooden box substantially wider than your window (see page 125 for instructions). Line the wooden box with a plastic one to make it easier to change the scheme later in the year.

PLANTS AND PLANTING

The plants can be set out in the window box as soon as all danger of frost has passed. Planting can begin two to three weeks earlier in the season if this can be done indoors. This allows the plants time to establish themselves before the box is placed outside. The initial size of the plants used can vary according to your budget. Small "plug" plants are inexpensive, but mature plants produce results much faster.

1 *Begonia* The multitude of bright flowers on this eye-catching plant are set off by its shiny green leaves. This tuberous-rooted begonia has good basal branching and is half hardy. It is reasonably priced and is best bought mature in the bud stage. Plunge into the box and, as its beauty fades, replace with another plant.

2 *Calibrachoa* 'Million Bells' A delicate, compact, petunialike plant that is covered in masses of dainty, pinkish-mauve blooms throughout the summer. The plant has good basal branching with a low trailing habit. Sturdy and weather resistant, the plants are not brittle and will stand up to a buffeting wind. If grown from small plants or cuttings, the centers should be pinched to encourage branching.

3 *Cuphea llavea* 'Tiny Mice' This spreading and slightly trailing plant forms a strong feature at the left of the box. The red and purple flowers, which look like small mice and give the plant its name, bloom for a long period.

4 *Helichrysum cymosum* This half-hardy plant sets off the front of the box with a mass of bright yellow flowers that are produced in profusion over a long period.

5 *Lilium* Many lily cultivars are available as dormant bulbs to be planted early and grown on before being set out in a window box. However, established, growing bulbs are available from many garden centers and supermarkets. As these will not last as long as other plants in the window box, it is best to plunge-plant the lilies still in their pots, so they can easily be replaced when they are past their best with either another lily or a different type of plant.

6 *Lobelia speciosa* 'Fan Scarlet' This half-hardy perennial, which flowers well

PLANT GALLERY

Two plants in this box are of particular interest and have only recently become available.

Cuphea llavea 'Tiny Mice': a native of Mexico and Brazil, its potential was spotted during an American plant breeding program. The flowers appear in abundance from late spring until the first frosts.

Monopsis 'Midnight': this beautiful South African plant will trail and cascade over the front of the box. The color and shape of the flowers give it the appearance of a trailing violet. It is weather resistant with fine feathery foliage.

from mid summer to early fall, is valuable in extending the flowering period of the planting. The spears of red flowers at the back of the box frame the soft yellow lilies. Lobelia can be grown from seed or bought as established plants. When the plants have finished flowering they should be taken in and given frost protection so they can be used the following year. Split each plant to create two or three new plants for next season.

7 *Monopsis* 'Midnight' This trailing plant spills over the front of the box with an abundance of blooms. The violet-blue flowers set off the deep reds and oranges of the other plants, enhancing the vibrancy of their colors.

8 *Nicotiana* x *sanderae* (Domino series) This lovely crimson selection of the flowering tobacco plant is a half-hardy annual and an excellent window box plant. Its flowers are upward looking and continue throughout the season.

9 *Petunia* Surfinia hybrids Unlike many other petunias, these hybrids are raised from cuttings. They are readily available from garden centers. Two colors are used in this box: a strong, deep purple and a rich burgundy.

10 *Tropaeolum majus* This sun-loving creeping plant twines itself through the other plants, its golden flowers brightening the front of the box.

CARE AND MAINTENANCE

Use a general purpose, soilless potting mix. In the height of summer, window boxes need watering frequently. Check by pushing a finger into the potting mix; it should feel moist at the heart of the box even if the surface is dry. Feed weekly with a general purpose liquid fertilizer.

cool summer color

This subtle planting is very different from the previous riot of color. The initial decision to make the box wider than the window is particularly successful here, as it allows the plants to be seen not only against the window but also against the mustard wall, which provides contrast for the pinkish mauves of the petunias and snapdragons. The creamy yellow tones create harmony and balance, softening the overall effect.

PLANT GALLERY
Passiflora citrina This is a recent addition to the plant catalogs. When used in a window box, it will need either a stake or some other form of support for it to be seen at its best

CONTAINER

The window box is the same as that for the "Vibrant Summer Color" (see pages 124–5 for instructions on constructing and fixing a box).

PLANTS AND PLANTING

If frost protection is available, the plants can be bought and established in early to mid spring. However, they should not be placed outside until all danger of frost has passed.

1 *Antirrhinum* 'Avalanche' This is a relatively new patio and window box plant—a true trailing plant with unusual silvery gray foliage and creamy, purple-flecked flowers. It is available from most garden centers as rooted cuttings or larger, more mature plants. Regular deadheading will ensure it blooms all summer.

2 *Sutera* 'Olympic Gold' (bacopa) A wide-spreading plant and an excellent trailer for the front of the container. The plant is covered with small, crisp white flowers, and the foliage is broadly margined in golden green. This plant is constantly in bloom from late spring to mid fall. It is best in sun or partial shade.

3 *Helichrysum petiolare* 'Gold' This excellent trailing plant adds a touch of bright foliage color and will last all summer.

4 *Tagetes erecta* 'Vanilla' A half-hardy annual, 'Vanilla' is the first white hybrid African marigold. With its large creamy white flowers and compact bushy habit, it forms a strong central focus in this planting scheme. It can reach a height of about 2 ft. (60cm), and will flower over a long period if deadheaded.

5 *Passiflora citrina* The lush leaves of this half-hardy climbing plant protect the delicate yellow flowers. The column of deep green forms an unusual feature in this summer window box. The plant has been plunged in its pot so that it can be removed easily for winter protection.

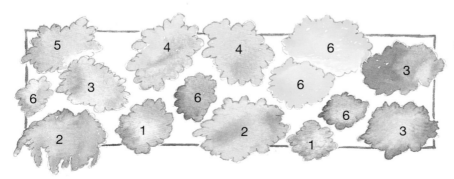

6 *Petunia* Surfinia hybrids No other plant provides such a reliable and outstanding show, regularly producing a wonderful cascade of color. The variegated bright mauve form used here adds a touch of contrast to the cream and yellow display, while the larger, yellow-flowered plant introduces a patch of brightness.

CARE AND MAINTENANCE

Use a general purpose, soilless potting mix with an added slow-release fertilizer. Liquid feed regularly, but not too frequently or the flowers will be swamped with an abundance of leaves. In hot weather, watering may be necessary as often as twice a day.

rich fall color

All three planting designs for this cottage window make full use of the colors that naturally accompany the changing seasons. As we have seen, the window is enhanced throughout the year with different planting schemes. The fall design includes a change of container color, too. The purple sets off the color of the plants, increasing the effect of the vibrant combination of strong colors.

PLANTS AND PLANTING

1 *Aster novi-belgii* (New York asters)
These plants bring a bright violet-pink to the scheme, lightening the tones where they nestle below the chrysanthemum and the viburnum. The bright yellow centers echo the color of the firethorn berries.

2 *Brassica oleracea* (ornamental cabbage)
The purple-pink center of this cabbage picks up the color of the aster flowers, and its crinkled foliage adds an interesting texture.

3 *Chrysanthemum* These large, multiflowered pot chrysanthemums are available in a wide range of colors. The orange-bronze shade used here is particularly appropriate for the season, and blends well with the color of the wall.

4 *Clematis* Petit Faucon 'Evisix' Blooming from mid summer to the fall, this nonclinging variety bears flowers of deep indigo blue with yellow anthers. A deciduous plant with a mature height of about 3 ft. (1meter), it tolerates any aspect but needs shade at the base of the plant. It prefers moist but not waterlogged soil.

5 *Lilium* 'Chinook' A beautiful, wide-petalled lily of a soft golden yellow heavily over-laid with orange. Its upright habit makes it a useful addition to the container, adding a strong vertical element to the planting. To get the maximum value out of this window box, the lily should be plunged in its pot into the potting mix so that it can be replaced with another plant once it has finished flowering.

6 *Perovskia atriplicifolia* (Russian sage) This plant has slender, silvery gray, aromatic leaves and waving spires of blue flowers that harmonize with the color of the clematis.

7 *Pyracantha* 'Orange Charmer' (firethorn) This yellow-berried form adds a touch of brightness to the front of the planting, where, spilling over the side, it stands out in strong relief against the purple window box.

8 *Viola* x *wittrockiana* This plant's dark, moody red adds depth and interest to the scheme, reinforcing the rich autumn colors. It combines with the viburnum foliage, setting up a vibrant contrast where it is outlined against the wall.

9 *Viburnum opulus* 'Sterile' A deciduous shrub with bright green leaves in the spring that turn red and burgundy in the fall. It needs regular pruning to stay compact enough for this type of window box.

CONTAINER

This display was planted up in a plastic trough (with drainage holes) that was then placed inside the repainted wooden window box.

CARE AND MAINTENANCE

Keep the potting mix just moist at all times, and feed the plants regularly with a high-potash fertilizer. The clematis stems need some support; thin sticks are most suitable.

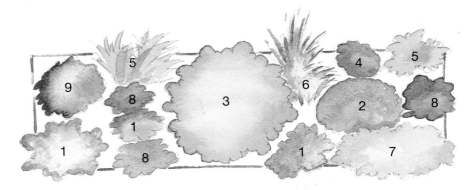

timeless classics

This chapter features both classical styles and reinterpretations of traditional favorites. The summer planting of pastel hydrangeas and gray-green baby's tears shown opposite displays the essence of this section. Classic simplicity of design and restrained use of color capture the spirit of the setting, and the cool marbled container is in harmony with the style of the traditional white balustrade.

In this chapter, the much-loved hanging basket filled with plants in simple combinations, or with the basics for a summer salad, becomes a modern classic. The handmade lead garland and bow decoration add an unusual festive twist, and cottage crackle pots bring easy seasonal planting schemes to a traditional cottage window.

hanging baskets

It is common to see hanging baskets filled with an abundance of flowering plants in a multitude of colors. They are an ideal setting for using the whole palette provided for us by the plant growers of today. However, there are other ways of planting the standard wire basket. There are also some attractive and unusual alternative basket designs.

summer blues

These hanging baskets (right) make a perfect pair, even though they were planted with different species. They balance each other because the plants were chosen for their similar color and form. The subtle differences in color and texture add interest to the display.

CONTAINERS

For good results, use a 16 to 18 in. (40 to 45cm) plastic-coated wire hanging basket. Smaller baskets do not allow the plants to become lush and abundant, and will also dry out quickly. Remember, though, that a basket should not be too big for the space in which it is to be displayed or it may overpower its surroundings.

Each basket was first lined with sphagnum moss then with black plastic. The plastic helps to keep in the moisture, and the moss, which disguises it, will disappear from view as the plants mature and spread.

PLANTS AND PLANTING

1 *Laurentia axillaris* (isotoma) 'Blue Star' This delicate summer hanging basket or patio plant is used in the right-hand basket. It forms a dome of feathery light mid-green foliage, which is wreathed with a myriad starlike flowers. They are bright lavender blue at the front and silvery white on the reverse. The plant forms mounds about 1 ft. (30cm) high and wide, making it perfect for hanging baskets.

2 *Scaevola aemula* This trailing plant, featured in the left-hand hanging basket, has lilac or lavender-blue flowers that are similar in shape to those of lobelia, but much larger.

CARE AND MAINTENANCE

Deadhead the plants on a regular basis and keep the potting mix moist at all times. Hanging baskets are very labor intensive at the height of summer; they require watering thoroughly at least once a day and feeding once a week with a high-potash liquid fertilizer. However, if this is done regularly they will continue to flower for three to four months.

straw cones

Hanging baskets are a gardening classic, and today there are ways to give a new twist to old favorites without losing their traditional appeal. For example, thanks to the introduction of different materials we no longer have to rely on the classic wire basket. Whatever its shape, the basket needs to be big enough to contain sufficient soil to anchor the plants and provide them with an adequate supply of water and nutrients.

CONTAINERS

These eye-catching baskets are made from slim bundles of dried grass attached to a strong, cone-shaped wire frame. They are lined with plastic to protect the basket from staining. If stored in a dry place over winter, these baskets should last for a number of seasons.

PLANTS AND PLANTING

1 *Begonia* x *tuberhybrida* 'Illumination White' This trailing begonia is particularly suited to hanging baskets as the large clusters of flowers hang down in such a way that they are best seen from below.

2 *Lobelia erinus* There are plenty of different strains of lobelia available in varying shades of mauve, lavender, white, and rose. Choose the trailing types for hanging baskets.

3 *Pelargonium* 'Maverick White' This large-headed bush pelargonium looks good all season. The flowers are surrounded by an abundance of lush green foliage.

4 *Pelargonium peltatum* 'Happy Face' Trailing 'Happy Face' has lovely pale pink flowers that last until the first frosts.

5 *Verbena canadensis* The purple-flowering plants were selected from the Olympia mixed strain. This plant's spreading, trailing habit makes it an excellent choice for hanging baskets

6 *Verbena* 'Tapien Violet Stripe' This trailing plant is well suited to hanging basket display. The attractive flowerheads are made up of clusters of individual flowers that have a bright lilac cross in the center.

CARE AND MAINTENANCE

Fill the cones with a soilless, hanging basket potting mix with some slow-release fertilizer added to supply nutrients. If watered at least every other day and in warm weather every day, these baskets should produce a profusion of wonderful flowers for two or three months. Although the potting mix contains slow-release fertilizer, it is still a good idea to give a weekly application of a high-potash liquid feed to ensure the plants stay strong and healthy. Deadhead regularly to remove any damaged or dying flowers.

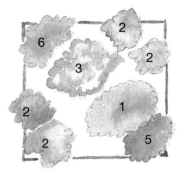

salad basket

There is no need to limit yourself to traditional hanging basket plants: experiment with unlikely plants and unusual combinations. This basket, which is not only beautiful but contains everything you need for a summer salad, shows how successful this strategy can be. Bright colors fill this "horn of plenty," and the glowing yellow and orange flowers of the marigolds and nasturtium set off the fresh greens of the salad leaves.

CONTAINER

This basket is made from the spent stems of the fruiting part of date palms, woven through a horn-shaped wire frame. It is lined with plastic to help retain water and to protect the basket from staining.

PLANTS AND PLANTING

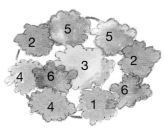

1 *Beta vulgaris* 'Rainbow Mixed' (chard) This plant was chosen for its crinkled, glossy leaves and colored stems. When planted in the garden chard makes large, spreading specimens, but seedlings and young plants are suitable for a short-term display in a container.

2 *Lactuca* (lettuce) The front of the basket is filled with several seedlings of a cut-and-come-again leaf lettuce called 'Salad Bowl'. It adds a fresh green to the basket and is delicious.

3 *Tagetes erecta* 'Vanilla' A yellow African marigold, used here for its value as a deterrent of aphids. Edible alternatives would be calendula, or pot marigolds.

4 *Thymus x citriodorus* 'Variegatus' This variegated thyme has a compact, bushy habit and its small leaves bring a change of texture to the basket. A few leaves of thyme give a real Mediterranean flavor to summer salads.

5 *Lycopersicon* (tomato) 'Bonsai hybrid' This trailing type is suitable for hanging baskets, and it bears cherry-sized fruit. 'Jolly hybrid' and 'Teardrop hybrid' are alternative varieties.

6 *Tropaeolum majus* The sun-loving nasturtium has edible leaves and golden yellow flowers. Young leaves and flowers add a spicy, peppery taste to mixed salads.

CARE AND MAINTENANCE

The basket is packed with plants that need to grow and develop, so it is essential that a slow-release fertilizer is added to the potting mix at planting time. A liquid feed should also be given once a week throughout the season. The tomato will produce fruit all summer, but as this is a very restricted space it is better to pinch it after two trusses to allow the fruit to develop and mature. Cut the leaf lettuce on a regular basis, but remember to leave enough to keep the plant healthy and looking good in the basket.

rococo tulips

Stunning plant displays can be created by focusing on a single design element, as with this beautifully simple scheme. The key to success is the use of repetition. A pleasing rhythm is set up by the pattern of the row of planters and the groups of tulips. This is echoed in the repeated lines of the fluting on the sides of the galvanized containers and in the pattern of horizontal lines of light and shadow cast by the shutters in the background.

The tulips and the planters make perfect partners: each echoes the curving shape of the other, and the sheen of the galvanized surface is similar to that of the natural bloom on the tulip petals. The plain white walls throw the rich color and shape of the tulips into relief.

CONTAINERS

The Rococo-style containers are an essential part of the design for this planting scheme. If you are unable to find identical ones, don't worry; you should be able to find something like them. Keep an eye out for other interesting and unusual containers that will provide inspiration for similar schemes.

PLANTS AND PLANTING

1 *Tulipa* 'Rococo' Tulips are one of the best spring bulbs to use for balconies or window boxes. The strong vertical line of the stem separates the solid, broad leaves at the base from the visually strong flowerheads at the top. This regimented effect can seem alien to a spring planting for a natural garden style but is just right for formal and semiformal settings such as this town balcony.

'Rococo' is a richly colored parrot tulip that has intriguingly fringed petals.

CARE AND MAINTENANCE

Once the shoots show above the surface, feed the bulbs with a liquid fertilizer once a week. Keeping the pot in a bright but cool position will extend the effective flowering period.

Deadhead the bulbs when the tulips have finished flowering; continue to water them while they die down naturally. In the fall the bulbs can be planted out in the garden where they may bloom the following year, although the flowers are likely to be smaller.

Tulips have a long flowering season and, if carefully chosen, will provide a succession of flowers for several weeks. Buy the bulbs in the fall and plant them in groups of between five and seven in 4 or 4 ¾ in. (10 or 12cm) pots. These should then be placed outdoors, preferably plunged into a bed of sand and insulated with straw or dry leaves. Starting with the early-flowering tulips, the pots that are ready can be plunged into an outer display container. After flowering, replace them with pots of other varieties to extend the season.

classic balcony

Framed by the distant hills, this scene is the essence of summer. Two simple but very different plantings make perfect partners for the white balustrade. Although cool summer colors are used for both containers, the shapes and textures produce very different effects. The harebells and lavender appear pastoral when compared to the bold shape of the hydrangeas. The container is painted with a delicate marbled finish in soft blues and grays that echo the rippling water behind.

hydrangea clouds

The beautiful view inspired this planting, which links the balcony with sea and sky. The soft pinks and powder blues of the flowers pick up the colors in the shrubbery glimpsed through the balustrade, and the forms of the flowerheads are echoed in the clouds and rolling hills.

Hydrangeas start off in soft, subtle shades and then, as the season develops, intensify in color to give the boldness that makes this container so eye-catching.

CONTAINER

The box is made from ½ in. (12mm) marine plywood (see page 125 for instructions). The

FLOWER COLOR
Hydrangeas can be made to turn a more intense blue by applying a soluble fertilizer containing an easily available form of iron, such as Sequestrene. Pink colors, on the other hand, can be made deeper and without lilac tones by adding a tablespoonful of lime to the watering can when watering.

exterior was "marbled" with emulsion paint, then sealed with three coats of matte exterior varnish. For the marbling, use colors that harmonize with the planting scheme.

PLANTS AND PLANTING

First set out the hydrangeas in irregular groups; this creates an interesting outline and allows the underplanting of baby's tears to be seen. Once you are happy with the position of the hydrangeas, fill in around them with potting mix. Plant the baby's tears between the hydrangeas; this carpeting plant will soon cover the soil surface.

1 *Hydrangea macrophylla* Hortensia form For containers these plants are best bought new each year—the old ones can be planted out in the garden. They can be planted directly in the window box, or plunged in pots into the planting mix so that they are easy to remove once the flowers have finished.

2 *Soleirolia soleirolii* (baby's tears) This is a plain, rich green form of baby's tears. The form

'Aurea' could be used in this design; it has very attractive lime-green foliage.

CARE AND MAINTENANCE

If possible, choose hydrangeas with a firm, sturdy habit. However, if the plants have been grown in a plastic tunnel or greenhouse they will be rather soft, and in this case each stem should be staked with a fine cane to prevent the wind breaking off the flowerhead. The color of hydrangea flowers is determined by the acidity of the potting mix (see "Flower Color," left). If you prefer a blue flower, use lime-free (ericaceous) potting mix; normal potting mix containing some lime will yield pink flowers. The natural environment for this type of hydrangea is open woodland; a position with dappled light suits them best and reduces the chance of the flowers being scorched by the sun. The baby's tears are also at home in this type of setting.

ALTERNATIVES

Changing the varieties of hydrangea chosen and altering the acidity of the growing medium will enable you to ring the changes with white or pink hydrangeas. Patio roses or miniature bush roses could be used to produce an overall similar effect to that of the hydrangea planting, though one with quite a different style.

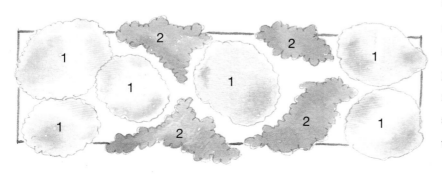

harebells and lavender

This scheme exploits the wonderful effect of simple plant combinations in which the focus is on the effect of the whole design rather than on the strong shapes and colors of individual plants. The ethereal quality of the harebells and lavender is quite different from that of the bold shape of the hydrangeas, and yet this scheme is equally successful and totally in keeping with the surroundings. The delicate colors and textures that are the special qualities of this planting make it seem an essential part of the scene. The fragile blue and mauve flowers hover on their stalks above the leaves as sunlight filters through, creating sparkling patterns of light and shade.

CONTAINER

The container is the same as that used for the hydrangea planting: a simple, plywood box given an attractive marbled finish.

PLANTS AND PLANTING

1 *Campanula medium* (Canterbury bells) Dwarf varieties of this bellflower reach a height of about 1 ft. (30cm) with a spread of 6 to 8 in. (15 to 20cm). They form clumps of foliage that are very suitable for growing in containers. Border varieties for the garden grow much taller.

2 *Campanula rotundifolia* The common harebell of European mountainsides produces delicate blooms on slender stems that last for three to four weeks. If the harebells are plunged in pots or planted in an inner liner they can be replaced after flowering.

3 *Lavandula angustifolia* (lavender) The misty gray-green stems and leaves give this

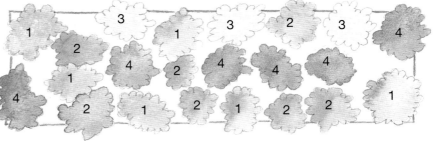

plant its delicate quality. Pale, beautifully scented flowers appear in mid to late summer on tall spikes held above the leaves.

4 *Lavandula angustifolia* The cultivar 'Hidcote' is an excellent, compact, stocky plant with dark blue flower spikes to add depth to the planting.

CARE AND MAINTENANCE

The whole of this display was first established with young plants in a plastic trough (with drainage holes) that fits within the outer box. It is important that lavender and harebells have good drainage, so place a 2 in. (5cm) layer of gravel in the plastic container before installing plants and potting mix. If an immediate effect is desired, established plants can be used.

All these plants like soilless potting mix and are best positioned in full sun. After flowering, cut off the dead flower spikes of the lavender and trim the plants to prevent them from becoming too leggy.

festive window box

Christmas is one of the few times of the year when we can indulge ourselves, decorating our home inside and out. Why not create a window box especially for the occasion, or embellish an existing one? This box has been decorated with easy-to-make lead garlands and bows that add a festive finishing touch. The colors of the plants were chosen to reflect the season, and the resulting display would bring a feeling of celebration to any entrance.

CONTAINER

The box should be large enough to allow the plants to be plunged into it while still in their plastic pots so as not to disturb their roots. This is particularly important for the holly, which was growing in large pots.

The box was made from marine plywood (see page 125 for instructions), then given a weathered look by painting it with a white matte undercoat that was overbrushed with a cherry-red outdoor wood preservative (use a brand that is safe for plants). The decoration was made from roofing lead cut into strips with the edges bent over to look like fabric swags; the strips were then tacked onto the box with panel pins. Wear protective gloves when handling lead.

SAFETY RULES

Lead can be handled perfectly safely if basic rules are followed and care is taken. Gloves should be worn at all times when handling lead, and hands should be washed thoroughly after working with it.

PLANTS AND PLANTING

1 *Cyclamen persicum* 'Cherry Red' Cyclamen are readily available in garden centers throughout the winter period; there are many different varieties, including several in rich, glowing reds such as this. The tuberous plants are not frost hardy, though they are happy in cool conditions and can be plunged into a window box for short periods of time to add seasonal color. They will survive outside in a frost-free area.

2 *Ilex* x *altaclerensis* 'Golden King' This golden variegated variety of holly will grow well in a container if it is properly looked after and fed regularly.

CARE AND MAINTENANCE

When plants are plunged, they need careful watering: each pot should be watered individually to avoid over- or underwatering. Be careful not to splash the tops of the cyclamen tubers, as this will cause them to rot. As the soil volume is restricted, the holly should be fed regularly with a balanced liquid fertilizer.

ALTERNATIVES

Ornamental cabbage would make an unusual addition to this bright, festive planting scheme, the color of the cabbage intensifying as night temperatures drop.

cottage crackle pots

This window sill gave us the opportunity to create something delicate and charming, but which still had all the impact of a well-designed scheme. The cottage window is very small, so it was important that the tall, crackle-finish pots helped to unify the scene by echoing the soft, creamy yellow walls, and that the planting be kept simple, to reflect the style of the cottage. The use of a pair of containers in this position was far more effective than using a single container set in the center of the window sill.

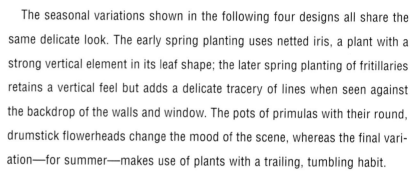

The seasonal variations shown in the following four designs all share the same delicate look. The early spring planting uses netted iris, a plant with a strong vertical element in its leaf shape; the later spring planting of fritillaries retains a vertical feel but adds a delicate tracery of lines when seen against the backdrop of the walls and window. The pots of primulas with their round, drumstick flowerheads change the mood of the scene, whereas the final variation—for summer—makes use of plants with a trailing, tumbling habit.

iris pots

CONTAINERS

The containers were bought from a garden center and are made from wood decorated with a crackle paint effect in a matte finish. They were intended to take dried materials for use indoors but will withstand being outside in a sheltered spot for two or three years. To make these pots suitable for planting outside, drill holes in the base and line them with plastic that has been punctured for drainage.

Flowering in early spring, species iris are charming flowers to use in simple displays in clay pots, in longer window boxes, or as they are here (right) in these upright containers. They are undemanding and easy to grow. Because of their delicacy they are best displayed on their own, so that the beauty of the individual flowers can be fully appreciated. Here, the window and surroundings act as a foil for the delicate flowers.

PLANTS AND PLANTING

1 *Iris reticulata* This rich purple-blue iris blooms in late winter and early spring, its flowers marked with splashes of gold. Corms are best bought in the summer or fall and planted in pots for flowering the following year. They are readily available from garden centers and also by mail order from specialist bulb dealers. When the time comes to replant the pots, put the iris in the garden where they will naturalize.

fritillary pots

Fritillaries have a subtle beauty. They are not brilliantly colored, but have a distinction and charm all of their own. Fritillaries are enjoying a great surge in popularity as people are introduced to some of the more unusual types, with their strikingly attractive flowers. The late spring planting shown overleaf uses two species and has a more delicate look than the iris pots, while keeping the vertical line that echoes the shape of the window.

PLANTS AND PLANTING

1 *Fritillaria acmopetala* Blooming in mid to late spring, this species is easy to grow in containers and can be naturalized in open, well-drained soil in most gardens after flowering. The wispy stems are about 10 to 12 in. (25 to

30cm) long, and crowned with three delicate flowers that last up to three weeks.

2 *Fritillaria meleagris* (snakeshead lily) The delicate, nodding flowers of this fritillary have an intriguing chequered pattern to the petals. There are several cultivars with flowers in varying shades of pink and purple. A white form is also available. The flowers are carried on stems 6 to 12 in. (15 to 30cm) tall.

primula pots

The white and lilac flowers of the drumstick primula (right) make a lovely display from mid to late spring. The clusters of flowers on a tall stem form a strong shape that works well with the angular form of the pots. These plants do not like to be disturbed, so plant them in plastic inner pots when young and put them into their final position as the flowerheads begin to show color.

The surface of the potting mix can be mulched with moss or gravel, which lends an attractive finish to the pots and helps retain moisture in the soil—an important consideration for these moisture-loving plants.

If you are planting up the crackle pots to provide a succession of color through spring and summer, the primulas can replace the fritillaries once the bulbs are past their best.

PLANTS AND PLANTING

1 *Primula denticulata* (drumstick primrose)
This perennial primula, related to the common
primrose and cowslip, is a beautiful addition to
the spring garden. The flowers occur in a range
of colors, from lilac to deep purple, and pale
rose to rich pink.

CARE AND MAINTENANCE

Drumstick primulas are relatively easy to grow,
and are happy in sun or partial shade, in moist
but not waterlogged soil. Use a general purpose,
soilless potting mix. As flowers fade, remove the
dead flowerheads. Division after flowering is
one of the easiest ways to increase your stock.
These plants thrive in pots or window boxes as
long as they are well watered; they soon wilt in
dry conditions.

summer pots

A cushion of trailing pale green and white foliage
smothered in vibrant purple-pink flowers makes
a sunny summer display. The undulating outline
of the plants' stems has been echoed by the
strong, wavy horizontal line of the drip trays,
which also act as water reservoirs and help
reduce the frequency of watering required in the
hot summer months.

PLANTS AND PLANTING

1 *Mesembryanthemum variegatum* 'Rose' This
is an excellent basket, pot, or patio plant. An
abundance of small, rose-pink, daisylike flowers
nestle among the leaves and appear in a long
succession throughout the summer.

CARE AND MAINTENANCE

A general purpose, soilless potting mix is suitable for all these plants. Some broken crocks in
the base will provide extra drainage if necessary.
The iris and fritillary are plants for the early,
cooler part of the year. Take care not to overwater them, but at the same time do not let the
soil mix dry out totally between waterings. The
mesembryanthemum is best in a bright, sunny,
sheltered spot. In hot conditions this plant may
need watering twice a day and will benefit from
being fed once a week with a high-potash liquid
fertilizer, such as tomato food. Position all these
plants—especially the fritillaries—where they
are protected from strong winds.

ALTERNATIVES

Portulaca, with its wide, brightly colored flowers
and fleshy leaves, and a growing habit that
makes it hug the containers, is a good alternative
trailing plant for this little window. The flowers
tend to open in waves over a long period, but it
does not thrive in wet weather.

fragrant balcony

Sitting out on a balcony on a summer evening is an idyllic way to spend a relaxing hour or two, particularly when the air is scented with the perfume of summer blooms. The flowers used in this planting give off their strongest scents in the evening, so that as dusk approaches you will find yourself enveloped in delicious fragrances. What better way could there be to wind down after a hard day's work? As in the best of gardens, this balcony is filled with an array of wonderful colors, shapes, and scents, pleasing our senses and rewarding our hard work. A clever arrangement of boxes of different sizes creates a staggered series of containers that overflow with plants.

If you are planting up a window box or balcony with perfume in mind, by all means use the usual floral favorites, such as roses, sweet peas, and lilies. But why not try some plants with richly perfumed foliage, too? Foliage can give fragrance to your boxes for much longer than most flowering plants, and often just brushing past the leaves will release wonderful aromas into the air. With a range of citrus-sharp, spicy, or musky perfumes, the scented-leaf pelargoniums used here are especially enjoyable.

CONTAINERS

This balcony display is composed of a series of marine plywood boxes, stained brown and arranged as cubes on top of one another. Three smaller planters are strategically placed to the front and side to create changes in levels.

The different sizes and staggered arrangement of the boxes allow the use of a variety of plant sizes, from the pot of sweet peas, which require deep, rich soil, to the smaller pots of pelargoniums and lavenders.

PLANT AND PLANTING

1 *Heliotropium arborescens* 'Marine'
This stocky plant has a rich, heady perfume. Its deep green leaves give solidity to the base of the group of plants, and the violet-blue flowers provide the perfect contrast to the pink of the roses and lilies, cooling down the color scheme. Heliotrope is a half-hardy annual with a long bloom period.

2 *Lathyrus odoratus* (sweet pea) There are hundreds of sweet pea varieties derived from the Spencer hybrids. All are beautiful and the

PLANT SUPPORT

Narrow bundles of thin branches make excellent natural supports for sweet peas. The bundles should be loosely bound with wire or twine and pushed into the soil in the containers before the sweet peas are planted.

majority have a strong perfume—seed catalogs usually tell you which are the best varieties for scent. The flowers should be picked every three or four days in order to encourage the plants to keep producing more, so you will have the bonus of perfume in the house. The sweet peas in the foreground of the photograph were grown in large plastic pots containing plenty of willow stems for them to climb up. If you have access to fresh willow, cut stems the previous winter and allow them to dry out. Alternatively, they can be bought from garden centers.

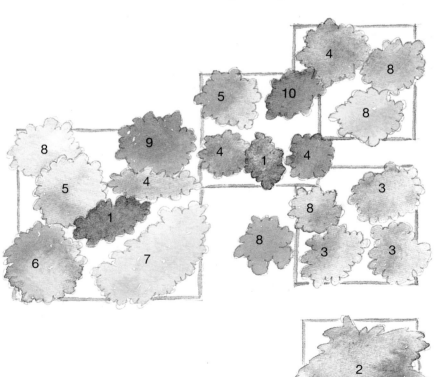

3 *Lavandula angustifolia* (lavender) This is a delicate plant in both structure and color. The pale pinkish lavender flowers are beautifully scented and will fill the balcony with their perfume from mid to late summer. The foliage is also aromatic, releasing its scent when the leaves are pinched between the fingers.

4 *Lavandula angustifolia* 'Hidcote' All the lavenders are worth including in this type of planting scheme; however, 'Hidcote' is one of the best. It is a short, stocky plant with spikes of deep blue flowers.

5 *Lilium* 'Montreux' This asiatic hybrid lily has a lovely light scent, but it is also used in the scheme for its color. The clear, fresh pink echoes the color of both the roses and the sweet peas in the foreground.

6 *Mentha* x *villosa* 'Variegata' (pineapple mint) This fragrant herb releases its fresh, fruity scent as one brushes past the foliage. The variegated leaves bring a touch of brightness to the lower corner of the boxes.

7 *Pelargonium* 'Candy Dancer' This plant has a similar habit and appearance to 'Lady Plymouth,' but with mid-green foliage and a beautiful rose-lemon scent. The species *graveolens* is similar in appearance and could be substituted here. Dozens of varieties of pelargonium are available from specialist nurseries and each brings something special to a planting.

8 *Pelargonium graveolens* 'Lady Plymouth' This scented-leaf pelargonium has deeply divided and serrated edges to its leaves that add to its beauty. The white and green variegation, coupled with the rose-mint smell, makes this a most attractive plant, although it is seldom included in fragrant designs.

9 *Rosa* 'Queen Elizabeth' This beautiful soft-to mid-pink floribunda rose dates from 1955 and is still one of the best roses around. Its very tall, upright habit makes it especially suitable for the back of a display; other plants can be strategically positioned in front to disguise its rather boring lower stems.

10 *Rosa* 'Pink Perpétué' A climbing rose with pink flowers of a deeper shade than 'Queen Elizabeth'. This adds height and reinforces the deep pinks at the back of the containers

CARE AND MAINTENANCE

Sweet peas need plenty of water and should be fed weekly with a tomato fertilizer if they are to remain productive. It is important to pick the flowers before they have a chance to form seed pods, as seed setting will prevent further flower production.

Deadhead the roses and other flowering plants, and pinch out the scented-leaf pelargoniums regularly to keep them bushy and prevent them from becoming straggly.

Sweet peas are best grown from seeds, which can be either sown in the fall and overwintered in a cold frame, or sown early in the spring, and hardened off before planting out. There are many varieties in a wide selection of colors, from white and cream through pink to dark reds and deep blues. The old-fashioned varieties often have a strong perfume though the flowers are usually smaller.

For sweet peas to bloom well throughout the season they should be planted in a deep container with plenty of rich potting mix. They are plants that reward a little care and attention, yielding a profusion of flowers and wonderful fragrance during the height of the summer, but they can be affected by the vagaries of the weather.

Early in the season, falling night temperatures over three or four nights can affect the plants by causing bud drop. The young flower buds, even if fairly well developed, simply fall off overnight. This does not happen once the night temperatures are constantly above 50°F (10°C). Regular watering during hot, dry weather encourages the growth of good, long flower stems, and also wards off the possibility of powdery mildew affecting the plants. A cool protected site and regular deadheading will see the plants flowering well into late summer.

formal box

All three schemes for this window box have a formal grace and are in sympathy with the style and proportion of the window, but each creates a very different effect. The white and green designs of the "Lily Garden" and "Formal Tulips" are based on traditional ideas of symmetrical styles of planting and have a very tranquil look. A similar symmetrical approach is taken for the design featuring red tulips, but here the fiery colors bring warmth and brightness to the scene.

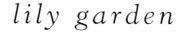

lily garden

The symmetry of the row of lilies adds a touch of grandeur to this window and, although the straight rows of plants have a strong structural look, the scheme softens the base of the window. This planting looks splendid from both inside and outside, and the lilies will fill the room with wonderful perfume when the windows are open. The design has been kept deliberately simple, with only two types of plant being used.

CONTAINER

This simple plywood window box was given a marble-effect finish. A plastic inner liner with drainage holes can be used to make it easier to change the plants after flowering.

PLANTS AND PLANTING

1 *Buxus sempervirens* 'Suffruticosa' (dwarf box) A versatile, easily grown, and readily available foliage plant, box is hardy to zone 5 as long as the roots are reasonably well protected. As the temperature drops, the foliage takes on some interesting hues, with gold and orange becoming more evident.

2 *Lilium longiflorum* (Easter lily) One of the most beautiful and striking of all the lilies, the clear, pure white of the large, trumpet-shaped flowers make it stand out from all others. It reaches a height of about 2 to 2 ½ ft. (60 to 75cm). If planting bulbs, you will require 8 to 12, depending on the size of the trough. Find four to six pots that are capable of taking two or three bulbs each when placed side by side in the trough. Fill the pots to about one-third full with soilless potting mix and sprinkle ½ in. (12mm) of sharp sand on top. Place the bulbs directly on top of this layer of sand, which will promote drainage and prevent the bulbs from rotting because of excess moisture. Continue to fill the pots with potting mix, making sure the bulbs' growing tips are just clear of the soil.

When the lilies are ready to open their buds, plunge them in their pots into the potting mix at the back of the trough. They will bloom for about three to four weeks after which they can be replaced with new plants.

When the planting is complete, finish off by covering the surface of the soil with medium-size green granite chippings.

CARE AND MAINTENANCE

Select good-sized, healthy lily bulbs and do not buy any that have moldy or mushy outer scales. This tall lily needs careful staking to withstand the vagaries of the weather. Keep the planting mix moist at all times throughout the growing season, without overwatering.

The plants will need to be changed on a regular basis to extend the flowering period. For a window box this size, six pots with three bulbs per pot should be used.

Because the box is permanently planted in this container, the potting mix will need additional nutrients supplied by top dressing with a balanced fertilizer in the spring. It will also need weekly feeding throughout the growing period. Box should be trimmed once a year in June.

ALTERNATIVES

If stronger color is preferred a range of alternative lily cultivars could be used. 'Yellow Connecticut King', 'Orange Enchantment', or 'Star Gazer' are just a few that would be suitable. Several of the newer, dwarf varieties, which usually do not need staking, could also be used.

flaming spring

This riot of color (right) will brighten up any early spring day. Formal in appearance, the rows of flowers in descending height make a spectacular display. This plant combination makes a striking contrast to the softer colors of the surroundings and proves that a timeless classic can combine vibrant color with a more traditional approach to design. This scheme should provide a display for about six weeks.

CONTAINER

To add some seasonal variation, a detachable facing can be added to the window box so that the color of the box can be changed to match changes in planting. (See page 125 for details.)

PLANTS AND PLANTING

The plants are grown in pots and transferred to the window box when ready to start blooming. Plunge the tulips into the potting mix in their pots so that they can be removed once flowering is over and other plants substituted to prolong the season of interest.

1 *Erysimum cheiri* These wallflowers were selected from the seedlings of an orange strain of 'Harlequin', but there are many strains of wallflower that will provide a burnt-orange to brick-red tone.

formal tulips

The strong shapes of the tulips work well with the formal setting of the window, their straight stems complementing the line of box plants that form a clipped hedge at the front. The soft white of the flowers and deep green of the the leaves and the box create a dramatic color contrast. Tulips, with their single, strong stems, are ideal for this type of formal scheme.

2 *Primula vulgaris* These bright red flowers with their cheerful yellow eye were selected from the Rapido strain of primroses, but there are many other strains that will provide flowers in this shade.

3 *Tulipa* 'Ile de France' A bright red, sturdy tulip growing to 20 in. (50cm) in height, with well-shaped flowers held on good strong stems.

4 *Tulipa* 'Queen of Sheba' This lily-flowered tulip is the taller of the two tulips used. It is an outstanding variety in a glowing orange-red, with long, straight stems that form a strong feature at the back of the planter.

PLANTS AND PLANTING

1 *Buxus sempervirens* 'Suffruticosa' (dwarf box) A neat, small-leaved evergreen fills the front of the box.

2 *Tulipa* varieties The large-flowered tulips used here are 'White Triumphator'. This variety has a beautiful cup-shaped head when in bud and through to maturity, but in the last stages of its flowering it develops a more open appearance, reminiscent of large white butterflies. The slightly shorter double tulip is 'Mount Tacoma'. As with the lilies, these tulips were plunged in pots into the back of the window box. The bulbs were planted in the fall with three to five bulbs in each pot; the pots were overwintered in a cold frame; in zones 4 to 6 store in a cold garage or cool closet. Once the shoots show through the soil, the pots can be brought into a cool room with plenty of light.

CARE AND MAINTENANCE

The box is tightly packed with four rows of plants, so care needs to be taken to ensure the potting mix does not dry out. A weekly application of liquid fertilizer will help keep the primroses flowering well and producing robust green leaves. The tulips can be replaced when they have finished flowering.

CARE AND MAINTENANCE

Keep the window box in a cool, sheltered position and make sure the planting mix is moist at all times. Occasional applications of a balanced liquid fertilizer will help keep the plants vigorous. Once the tulip flowers are over, remove the pots of bulbs and continue to water them until the leaves die down. The bulbs can then be taken out and dried, ready for planting out in the garden in the fall.

pure and simple

The aim of these planting schemes is to give the appearance of having been put together with effortless ease. At the heart of all the designs are simple but clever ideas, subtle color combinations, and uncomplicated planting, but this simplicity of approach does not mean less impact—on the contrary, all these plantings are very striking. Don't be afraid to go ahead with a really simple idea; you will discover that the plainest design can have the most dramatic effect.

Look at the "Country Garden" to see how effective a natural approach to planting can be, creating a tapestry of subtle colors. For a truly minimalist planting follow the example of "Seaside Simplicity," a perfect illustration of an impressive single-plant scheme.

seaside simplicity

This wonderful location on a small balcony by the sea needs little dressing up. Plants and containers used in a situation such as this must highlight their surroundings and not act as a distraction. The two very simple designs for the balcony enhance the setting and lead the eye through to the beautiful view. Understated containers combined with single-subject planting schemes show clearly that in some settings less is definitely more.

summer reds

The slightly larger spaces afforded by balconies give us the opportunity to use bigger groups of pots and other containers, and to experiment with plants with architectural qualities, such as the crocosmia used here. Its upright wands of flame red flowers, bold, straplike leaves, and the sculptural, arching stems help enhance the view without in any way obscuring it.

CONTAINERS

Large terracotta pots such as these are readily available, but in cold areas make sure they are frost proof if they are to stand out all year. Look out for pots that have interesting shapes, but avoid designs that are too fussy.

PLANTS AND PLANTING

1 *Crocosmia* 'Lucifer' This striking plant grows from a corm, but is usually available as a growing plant in a pot from most garden centers. It will reach around 5 ft. (1.5m) high. Crocosmia establishes itself in the garden very easily and can become invasive. When the plant needs to be divided, it can be broken up into small sections and replanted.

CARE AND MAINTENANCE

To get the most out of the large terracotta pots, the crocosmia should be replaced by another plant as its season comes to an end. For this reason, it is best to grow it in a plastic pot slipped inside the terracotta one, making the changeover easy. Use a general purpose, soilless potting mix, and keep this just moist at all times. Occasional feeding with a balanced liquid fertilizer helps prolong the flowering season.

ALTERNATIVES

Lobelia 'Queen Victoria' has dark red foliage as well as a vibrant red flower spike. It blooms over a long period and can be planted in the container once the crocosmia has finished.

fall white

CONTAINERS

For this display the chrysanthemums were left in their plastic growing pots, the outsides of which were simply wrapped in lengths of roofing lead cut from a roll. This is available from builders' merchants, is very malleable and can be bent into shape easily.

The dense growth of the chrysanthemums can make it difficult to water the pots; if this is the case, the pots can be taken out of the lead casing and plunged into a bucket of water every three days or so as necessary, depending on the weather. They should then be drained and replaced inside the lead cylinders.

Lead weathers well, taking on a soft, dull patina that looks attractive with most plant combinations. It is the simplicity of the dome of massed white flowers set against the straight lines of the lead casing that makes this uncomplicated scheme so effective.

PLANTS AND PLANTING

1 *Chrysanthemum* cultivars There are numerous cultivars of garden chrysanthemums, most of which are moderately hardy. The types used here are the multiflowering ones with dense rounded shapes and abundant small flowers (sometimes known as the Charm strain).

Varieties include white 'Casablanca'; there are also golden, pink, and red forms.

CARE AND MAINTENANCE

The chrysanthemums are best bought in tight bud; the buds will develop and open over a period of about a week, and the flowers will last for up to five or six weeks. The plants must be watered regularly—if they are allowed to flag before watering they will develop a kink in the stems and the flowers will not be shown off to their best advantage. The pots are tightly packed with roots making frequent watering a must, particularly in sunny or windy weather. Add a high-potash liquid fertilizer to the water once a week.

The plants should be brought in for the winter before frosts occur to spoil the flowers. If you have a greenhouse it is very easy to take cuttings in the spring from one of these over-wintered plants so you can increase the stock for future years.

ALTERNATIVES

During the spring, white azaleas could be used with great success. A different plant to try for the fall season would be colorful asters such as the New York variety.

SAFETY RULES

Lead can be handled perfectly safely if basic rules are followed and care is taken. Gloves should be worn at all times when handling lead, and hands should be washed thoroughly after working with it.

summer kitchen garden

A window box does not always have to be positioned directly beneath a window; here the space was a rather awkward one between two windows. The worn weather-boarded walls and simple windows proved to be the perfect

background for these culinary window boxes. It is always very important to look at the textures and materials of the walls and windows when choosing the style of window box and the plants to fill it. Here, the rough-sawn timber of the box blends perfectly with the background.

strawberries and herbs

The setting for this box, and the choice of plants, conjures up a real summer vacation feeling—and there is nothing nicer than picking your own strawberries or gathering a bunch of fresh herbs for a summer salad.

CONTAINER

The window box needs to have the same rustic appearance as the time-worn walls. Pull apart an old wooden pallet—or use weather-beaten boards—and assemble the box with gaps in between the slats to allow for planting. (See

page 126 for construction details.) This box was then very lightly brushed with dilute white matte emulsion paint to give an aged effect. The whole thing took no more than two hours to make before it was ready for planting.

PLANTS AND PLANTING

Most of the plants in this box are fairly hardy, but for best results they should not be planted out until late spring.

1 *Allium schoenoprasum* (chives) This onion relative thrives on being cut back often. Its purple, drumhead flowers are edible.

2 *Fragaria* x *ananassa* (strawberry) A number of cultivars can be used for this type of display. The season can be extended by growing early- and late-fruiting varieties in separate containers so that they can be plunged into the window box at the appropriate time. If you do not have a place to grow different varieties before they go into the window box consider perpetual varieties such as 'Gento', or summer and autumn alpine strawberries such as 'Baron Solemacher'. A good all-round, mid-season variety is 'Cambridge Favourite'. Plants can be bought from a garden center or by mail order.

3 *Mentha rotundifolia* 'Variegata' (pineapple mint) An invaluable herb for every cook, the foliage of this variegated mint will last well into the fall. If you would like to keep the plant compact, then trim the shoots throughout the season; for a trailing effect over the edge of a box, leave some of the stems uncut.

4 *Salvia officinalis* 'Icterina' (sage) This variegated sage is not quite as hardy as the plain one. The flavor is milder but still distinctive. Keep trimming the plants season long to prevent them from becoming leggy. Harvest and dry sage leaves for winter use.

5 *Thymus* (thyme) There are numerous varieties of thyme, so there is one to suit almost any location. Choose a form with a small leaf and pretty flowers for use in a container. As with several of the herbs in this display, the plants will need regular trimming to keep them compact and tidy.

6 *Origanum vulgare* 'Aureum' (golden marjoram) The small yellow leaves of the golden form of marjoram add a bright splash of color to the box. The aromatic flowers produced in mid summer are useful for garnishes, while the leaves can be used for salads and stuffing.

CARE AND MAINTENANCE

This planting is intended to be semipermanent and will require good nutrition to develop and flourish. Add a sprinkling of slow-release fertilizer to an open-textured, soilless potting mix to fill the box, and ensure there is free drainage. These plants are fairly hardy, but for best results do not place the planted box outside until late spring. In a hot, sunny site watering will be needed at least twice a week, and all the herbs will benefit from frequent cutting back. Cut off any runners from the strawberries, and either discard them or plant them in the garden. Runners taken from parent plants in late summer can be rooted and grown on to provide replacement plants for the following year.

PLUNGING

The beauty of a window box can be maintained for much longer by plunging plants in separate pots into the potting mix. The season for this box can be greatly extended by replacing the strawberry plant as it finishes fruiting; start off with an early-fruiting variety, then change to a mid-season and finally a late-fruiting type. For a colorful fall touch, replace the strawberry with a hot pepper: good cultivars for this type of planting are 'Cayenne' or 'Fiesta'. If you prefer sweet peppers, plant compact varieties such as 'Sweet Pickle' or 'Jingle Bells'.

salad bowl

This is another clean, crisp planting that not only brightens the view, but also contains all the ingredients for a summer salad. The lovely range of fresh green leaves and the interesting variety of textures provide simple ingredients that combine to make a beautiful display. The whole scheme has been designed to be an integral part of this summer scene. The marigolds add a bright flash of color to the subtle greens and also help keep aphids at bay.

CONTAINER

The simple, white box provides a perfect background for the fresh, green hues of the salad vegetables and herbs.

PLANTS AND PLANTING

1 *Allium fistulosum* (Welsh onion) A clump-forming plant with broad leaves and a good flavor, this is excellent cut into salads.

2 *Allium tuberosum* (garlic chives, Chinese chives) This clump-forming plant grows to about 10 to 12 in. (25 to 30cm) in height. The

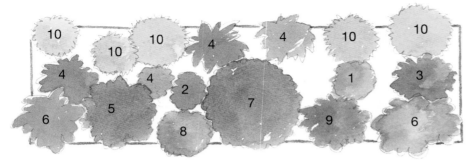

aromatic leaves are available for picking throughout the season.

3 *Anethum graveolens* (dill)   Small seedlings are used in this window box and are replaced on a regular basis—mature plants would be too large for this position. The feathery, fragrant foliage is used in salads and fish dishes.

4 *Beta vulgaris* 'Rainbow Mixed' (chard) The leaf stems of this ornamental vegetable appear in a range of bright colors. For this box seedlings with red stems were chosen, but depending on the color scheme, orange-, yellow-, or white-stemmed plants can be used.

5 *Lactuca* 'Lollo Rossa' (lettuce) A green and red, cut-and-come-again lettuce for cropping throughout the season. The leaves form a strong rounded head with good lasting qualities.

6 *Lactuca* 'California Mesclun Mix' (lettuce) A mixture of salad-green varieties grown for cutting as seedlings on a regular basis.

7 *Ocimum minimum* (bush basil) The compact, bushy form of this small-leaved plant

adds interest to the center of the box. It is a half-hardy annual needing warmth and shelter.

8 *Petroselinum crispum* var. *neapolitanum* (flat-leafed parsley) Also known as French or Italian parsley, this is a strong-flavored form that is delicious added to green salads.

9 *Raphanus sativus* 'Flamiuil' (radish)   An improved French breakfast type. It combines good holding qualities with a lovely flavor and an attractive white and brilliant red color.

10 *Tagetes erecta* 'Vanilla' This creamy African marigold flowers early and has a compact habit, growing to about 1½ ft. (40cm) high. African marigolds are not edible but they contain a naturally occurring chemical that helps to deter aphids, thus keeping your lettuces clean. Edible calendula, or pot marigold, could be used as an alternative. Its petals can be used in salads, as can those of 12-inch-tall 'Lemon Gem' signet marigold.

CARE AND MAINTENANCE

Keep the plants well watered and feed them at least once a week with a balanced liquid fertilizer. Deadhead the marigolds as required, and remove dying or faded foliage as necessary. You may need to take precautions against slugs, which will be attracted to the lettuce; there are various environmentally friendly controls and deterrents available.

late season color

Fall presents us with such a glorious array of colors and textures that it is sometimes hard to decide which ones should be included in a display. In summer, flowers dominate, but at this time of year leaves, bark, and berries really come into their own along with the late-season blooms.

CONTAINER

This simple but effective box is made from ½ in. (12mm) marine plywood. Measure your window area and cut the plywood to size. The box must be big enough to take plants that have been container grown in 1¾ or 2½ pint (1 or 1.5 liter) pots; a width and depth of around 6 in. (15cm) should be suitable. Paint the box with waterproof wood finish inside and out, and line the interior with black plastic (an empty potting mix bag or garbage bag is suitable). Cut holes in the base of the bag for drainage. The finished box is covered with a natural willow fencing material, available from garden centers (see page 126 for instructions on decorating the container).

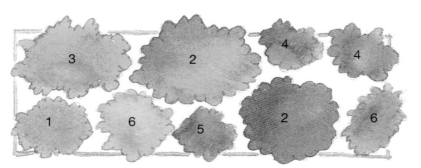

PLANTS AND PLANTING

1 *Buxus sempervirens* 'Suffruticosa' (dwarf box) A neat plant with small round leaves. Although it is evergreen, it often develops lovely fall tints of beige and brown.

2 *Chrysanthemum* Pot chrysanthemums are wonderful plants for adding masses of color to a display. Because they are so inexpensive, they can be removed and discarded when the flowers are over, and replaced with another plant just coming in to bloom.

3 *Cotoneaster* These berry-bearing plants are tremendous value. There are several compact species that are suitable for a window box, including *C. adpressus*, *C. congestus* 'Nanus', and *C. conspicuus* 'Decorus'. Some of these have a spreading, trailing habit that would cascade over the edge of the box.

4 *Photinia* x *fraseri* This is a vigorous evergreen shrub that would be suitable for a window box for a fairly short time. Its young leaves have lovely coppery bronze tones.

5 *Stephanandra incisa* An attractive plant with slender branches and delicate leaves that turn golden yellow in the fall. This is an easy plant to grow. Here it adds a delicacy to the planting in front of the chrysanthemums.

6 *Weigela florida* 'Variegata' This deciduous shrub will lose its leaves in the fall, but while they persist they form an attractive addition to the box, marked as they are with pale green and gold, often with a pink tinge.

CARE AND MAINTENANCE

The foliage plants act as a framework for the chrysanthemums that have been plunged into this container, and could be replaced later on by pots of fall-flowering bulbs.

dressed-up bay trees

The traditional style of this town balcony is complemented by the simple formality of a pair of clipped bay trees. These trees have a classic charm, but their form is strong enough to take a little dressing up. The addition of some

flowering plants around the base of the trunks adds a lively twist to the scene with a bright splash of color. This brings some welcome seasonal variety without detracting from the simple line of the trees and the unusual pots.

spring dressing

For the spring and early summer, bright yellow wallflowers give a cheery feeling with their warm color, bringing a patch of sunlight to the scene. Their spicy fragrance will linger around the doorway and lift the spirits.

CONTAINERS

These terracotta pots are frost resistant, so are suitable for year-round use outdoors except in very cold areas. Other containers for this type of planting would be those made from lead, or classic wooden Versailles tubs.

PLANTS AND PLANTING

1 *Laurus nobilis* (sweet bay) This classic culinary bay has the added advantage of supplying the kitchen with deliciously pungent fresh bay leaves. It is best to buy these trees grown to the size and shape you require; they are expensive to purchase, but worth the cost if they are well looked after.

They will need regular watering and feeding. To keep their shape they need to be trimmed back several times during the summer; the shoots cut off will provide leaves which can be dried for use in stews and casseroles.

2 *Erysimum cheiri* (wallflower) Cross-shaped flowers with rounded, oblong petals appear in clusters at the end of stems 1 to 1½ ft. (30 to 40cm) in length. Available in a really wide range of colors, these flowers have a strong, rich perfume. The yellow tones of the wallflowers used here pick up the creamy yellow flowers of the bay trees; the variety is 'Golden Yellow' but there are lots of other cultivars in similar shades, such as 'Cloth of Gold', from which to choose.

The wallflowers were grown in plastic pots through the winter and early spring and plunged into the planter as they came into bud. Growing a range of plants in pots in this way would allow a whole succession of different spring flowers to be used to enhance these containers.

AGING TERRACOTTA
To age any terracotta container, wash or brush the surface with a weak solution of animal manure or milk. The solution will soak into the porous surface of the pots and encourage the establishment of algae and mosses, which will quickly mellow pots and take away the rawness of the surface.

CARE AND MAINTENANCE

Use either a soil-based potting mix or a soilless mix with some grit added to give a free-draining growing medium with body and weight. Bay requires well-drained conditions, but needs plenty of water during the growing season. It responds well to regular feeds with a balanced liquid fertilizer.

Bay trees will withstand a certain level of frost, but more than a few degrees will damage the foliage and spoil the appearance of formal specimens like these. If a heavy frost is expected, the plants can be protected by draping them with bubble wrap or similar material. Alternatively, north of zone 8 overwinter the trees in a frost-free conservatory.

ALTERNATIVES

Classic mop-headed bay trees have been used for this planting; however, a number of more elaborate shapes is available. In very cold regions where bay trees would be damaged by the winter temperatures, other plants can be used to create the same effect.

A good alternative is topiary English holly, which is hardy to zone 6; however, it is a more expensive plant and slower growing than bay. Another classic topiary subject is the English yew, *Taxus baccata*; the cultivar 'Fastigiata' has a natural upright habit.

summer dressing

The color changes from spring gold to warm red in summer as the planting is changed from wallflowers to wax begonias. The rich color of the flowers and leaves harmonizes beautifully with the terracotta of the pots and brings a touch of summer heat to the balcony.

PLANTS AND PLANTING

1 *Begonia semperflorens* Raising these plants from seed is possible though quite difficult for the home gardener, and most people purchase begonias as ready-to-plant summer bedding plants; they are freely available and good value. The fleshy leaves may be a strong, bright green or an attractive bronze shade, depending on the variety. Flower color ranges from white through pink and salmon up to a strong red, and flowers are produced in profusion throughout the summer, particularly if the plants are fed once a week with a high-potash liquid fertilizer.

ALTERNATIVES

For a permanent planting around the base of the bay trees try dwarf box (*Buxus sempervirens*). This small-leafed evergreen plant is an ideal subject for basic topiary work and could be clipped into a neat shape, in keeping with the formal style of the setting.

CARE OF BAY TREES
Bay trees in containers need to be well looked after. Top dressing in the spring, with a mixture of slow-release fertilizer and potting mix, and regular watering and feeding, will keep them looking good throughout the year. Because bay trees are only moderately frost tolerant there can be a problem if they are used in cold areas. In this situation the pots must either be taken into a frost-free environment or wrapped in commercial horticultural fleece, which will provide protection from a few degrees of frost.

country garden

A freer, wilder approach to planting has been used for these window boxes, creating a gentler, more natural look. The result is an overflowing tapestry of texture and color with the unkempt charm of a country garden. These window

boxes, so perfectly suited to their rural surroundings, would work equally well in a town setting, where they would add the touch of a country meadow to an urban environment.

meadow tapestry

There is a style of garden design called tapestry planting, in which plants of many different colors and varieties are combined to create a complex yet unified picture, just like a fabric tapestry. Surprisingly, perhaps, this style of planting can easily be adapted for window boxes: a simple window with a good sunny aspect would lend itself perfectly to such a design. The effect is most successful when all the flowers are approximately the same size, helping to build up a richness of texture and create the true tapestry effect.

CONTAINER

The box was made from ½ in. (12mm) marine plywood painted with plant-safe wood preservative. The bottom had ½ in. (12mm) holes

PLANTS FOR
TAPESTRY SCHEME
Select plants that will bear a profusion of small flowers and have a multibranched habit, so that they can intermingle and weave together, creating a meadow carpet covered with a plethora of flowers. The tapestry style requires the individual plants to be positioned closely together; this dense planting takes a great deal out of the potting mix over a season. Regular liquid feeding at least once a week is essential.

drilled along its length for drainage. The basic box was then covered with natural willow fencing material bought from a garden center (see page 126 for instructions on decorating the container). The willow was attached horizontally so that it could be bent around the sides of the box and secured with panel pins. An ordinary, inexpensive plastic trough containing the potting mix and the plants was then concealed inside the window box.

PLANTS AND PLANTING

A few weeks before the display is required, the plants should be planted in a plastic trough that will fit inside the window box. Keep the trough in a greenhouse or similarly protected position until the plants are well established and coming into flower, then insert the plastic trough into the outer container for an instant effect.

1 *Brachycome* (Swan River daisy) Beautiful, small, starlike, daisy flowers in white, yellow, or blue are set in a fine tracery of feathery, mid-

green foliage. These plants will tolerate light shade, but they bloom best in full sunlight.

2 *Lobelia valida* This fairly new addition to the range of patio, container, and window box plants is set to become a "must have." The erect, bushy form of this lobelia is very appealing. The stems are topped by small, clear-blue flowers that last and last—an excellent low-maintenance plant.

3 *Sutera cordata* 'Snowflake' (bacopa) The stems of this trailing plant cascade over the front of the window box, with small white flowers set among light lime-green foliage.

4 *Sisyrinchium striatum* This is used at the back of the box to give height. Though better suited to moist or even boggy conditions, this plant will tolerate life in a container as long as it is watered frequently. It has a strongly vertical, straplike leaf and the upright flower spike is wreathed in tiny, creamy yellow flowers.

CARE AND MAINTENANCE

This box is packed with plants, so frequent and regular watering will be necessary. An application of high-potash liquid fertilizer once a week will help sustain flowering through the season.

After the first flush of flowers on the Swan River daisy, lightly trim just behind the old flowerheads, being careful not to cut off the other buds still to come.

cottage garden

A different interpretation of the natural look uses a taller planting scheme to re-create a traditional cottage garden in miniature, with all the range of color and shape associated with this well-loved garden style. A fine tracery of delicate flowers softens the window and creates a frame for the view from within the room. A window box should always be designed to be seen from both the inside and the outside of a window—a point often missed by gardeners.

PLANTS AND PLANTING

1 *Aquilegia* 'Long Spurred hybrids' A traditional cottage garden plant with fine, long stems holding delicate nodding heads. This hardy perennial flowers from early to mid summer and can also provide cut flowers for the home.

2 *Centranthus ruber* (Jupiter's beard) This attractive, pale pink form of the short-lived perennial is soon past its best in a window box, though delightful while in flower. Discard leggy plants after flowering. *Centranthus* self-seeds in the garden very readily.

3 *Argyranthemum frutescens* (marguerite daisy) A branching, woody-stemmed perennial with masses of bright, butter-yellow, daisylike flowers and finely cut foliage. The plants are tender and should be overwintered under cover in cold regions: cuttings root easily when taken in spring. There are several different cultivars in a range of delicate colors.

4 *Tamacerum parthenium* (feverfew) A true cottage garden plant that produces a series of small daisylike flowers with a yellow center circled by a row of white petals. The flowers are set on long stems among fine, pierced, aromatic foliage of a fresh, light green.

5 *Francoa sonchifolia* (bridal wreath) A tender perennial plant with deeply cut foliage and long wands of pinkish-white flowers that last a long time. In cold winter areas pot it up and overwinter in a greenhouse or sunroom.

6 *Sumatra jamesbrittenia* 'Indigo' A trailing and tumbling plant, its soft pink flowers and fine leaves add a delicacy that contrasts with the argyranthemum in the center of the box. It has a long flowering season.

7 *Penstemon* cultivars A beautiful summer perennial, penstemon has a foxglove type of flower that brings a vertical element to the back of the planting. Many different varieties are available in numerous shades of red, pink, and carmine as well as the white one used here. Penstemon is easily propagated from cuttings throughout the year.

8 *Veronica spicata* An easily grown perennial with erect racemes of flowers in shades of pink and rich blue, that stand like spires above the fine leaves. The plant is about 2 ft. (60cm) tall.

9 *Viola* Wink series This pretty blue and white pansy adds color at the base of the planting scheme. It flowers over a long period with a profusion of blooms.

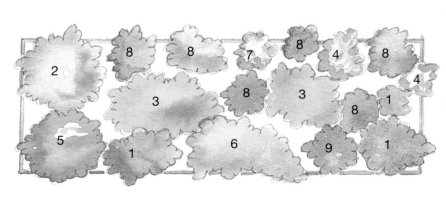

galvanized trough

A clever combination of simple planting schemes with a galvanized trough creates these modern designs that are perfect for a city balcony or window. The setting is one of the most important factors to take into account when selecting plants and planter. Unusual and satisfying effects can be produced when the background is treated as an integral part of the design. Texture is a strong element in the planting schemes for this trough. Rocks or pebbles can be used along with plants to create interesting textural contrasts. Keep an eye out for other unusual containers that will give an individual, modern twist to your window garden. Always ensure that it will be possible to punch drainage holes in the base of any container to be used for growing plants.

tulip field

Plant growers generally aim to produce new cultivars with bigger, bolder, and more colorful flowers, but the species plants from which the new cultivars are derived can give us a lovely contrast to the large flowers we so often see. This is definitely the case with spring bulbs, particularly tulips. There are a number of species that have a lovely, delicate appearance and the true beauty of the flowers is seen in full sun, as the petals open to reveal their gorgeous centers.

The bright pink species tulip set against the white walls and balustrade is very striking. Its narrow, blue-green leaves create a wonderfully spiky pattern against the slats of the window shutters, and their color is reflected in the galvanized metal container.

CONTAINER

This galvanized metal trough needed to have drainage holes punched in the base. The holes should then be covered with a thick layer of coarse drainage material.

PLANTS AND PLANTING

1 *Tulipa humilis* This narrow-leafed species tulip is a delicate addition to the spring garden. The rich pink flowers are about ½ in. (2cm) across, and the overall plant is 2 to 4 in. (5 to 10cm) high. It is particularly effective when planted in a block. The shape of the flowers contrasts with the long, narrow leaves, creating a dramatic effect.

CARE AND MAINTENANCE

Tulips are best put in containers or the open garden in mid fall. Set them 3 to 4 in. (8 to 10cm) below the soil surface; the deep trough used here allows them space to develop a good root system. After flowering let the leaves die down naturally, then lift the bulbs and dry them out. Store them in a dry place with good air circulation, ready for later replanting. Species tulips can be left in their pots, but the potting mix must be very free draining if they are to do well.

winter color

The trough has been placed on a low wall near a window so that it can be seen in all its glory, bringing a touch of brightness to dull winter days. The cushion of rich color and texture spills over the side of the trough, creating a striking

contrast to the shiny metallic surface. This type of mass planting with multiples of a single species can produce dramatic effects.

PLANTS AND PLANTING

1 *Primula vulgaris* These plants were selected from the Wanda strain. This very popular and reliable commercial strain, bred from the English primrose, has quilted green foliage with the leaves at the center of the plant taking on burgundy to maroon tones that are echoed by the deep, rich color of the flowers with their contrasting yellow eye. This strain of primula is hardy to zone 5.

CARE AND MAINTENANCE

Hybrid primroses are not difficult to grow from seed, but established plants are cheap to buy and readily available. Buy them when they are just starting to show a little color in the flower buds. Once the flowers are over, the primroses can be planted out in the garden. They do best in light shade with damp soil.

ALTERNATIVES

Winter pansies are available in a wonderful range of colors, but for a pretty foliage effect that will last all winter even in hard frosts, plant with *Arum italicum* or a mixture of *Arum italicum* and snowdrops (*Galanthus nivalis*).

modern verbascum

Here, minimalist planting complemented by the strong outlines of the galvanized container and vertical cones produces a striking but easily maintained display. The success of this scheme relies on the contrasting textures of the metal trough, the blue-gray slate "pennies," and the pale, velvety verbascum leaves. The laurentia (isotoma), with its light, open form and feathery texture, brings an element of contrast to the more solid shapes. The galvanized cones add a strong sculptural element; they can be obtained from florists and are simply speared into the compost. The finishing touch is given by soft blue slate pennies and granite chippings on the surface. These not only set off the textures of the plants, but also act as a moisture-retaining mulch.

PLANTS AND PLANTING

1 *Santolina chamaecyparissus* (lavender cotton) The silver foliage of this plant gives a fine, feathery contrast to the solid leaves of the verbascum. It brings a lightness to the base of the galvanized cones.

2 *Laurentia axillaris* (isotoma) An abundance of attractive, starlike blue flowers make this plant a good choice for the patio or container. It is a relatively recent introduction but is quickly becoming very popular and is readily available from garden centers.

3 *Linaria* 'Blue Lace' A delicate plant with tiny little blue flowers carried among silvery gray foliage on trailing stems.

4 *Verbascum bombyciferum* A stunning plant with large, pointed leaves densely covered in soft, silver velvet. A real eye-catcher in any plant display, it likes a sunny, open position.

CARE AND MAINTENANCE

Use an open-textured, soilless potting mix, filling the container to within about 1 in. (2.5cm) of the rim to allow space for watering. Place the container in a sunny position, keep the potting mix moist (but never wet), and feed regularly with a balanced liquid fertilizer. Take care not to splash the furry verbascum leaves.

The verbascum is a biennial, and so will last well in this display for the whole season. At the end of the year the plant should be taken out of the container and planted in the garden: during its second year it throws up a stately flower spike up to 7 ft. (2 meters) high.

no problem places

Shady corners, windy terraces, and damp mossy walls are all areas that you may want to brighten with an interesting window box but that can pose real problems for the plants. Even warmth and bright sunshine can be a problem for plants on a dry, baking-hot wall exposed to the glare of the sun. There are solutions to all these problems as long as you work with the conditions, choosing plants that not only tolerate these locations, but positively thrive in them.

In this chapter you will find designs that turn a disadvantage into an asset. A beautiful woodland box brings color to a shady corner, and on a roof terrace sculptural grasses and sedge create an unusual focal point with their wonderful textures and graceful movement.

hot spots

Most people love the idea of warm sunshine, but a really hot, sunny spot can be very difficult for plants in window boxes or other containers. The answer is not to fight against the conditions but to find plants that positively thrive in them. The two planting schemes shown here offer very different solutions to the problem. One uses cacti to present an image of the extreme conditions of the burning desert; the second is more Mediterranean in feel, featuring gray- and silver-leafed plants that are so well suited to dry conditions.

cactus garden

A touch of the desert comes to window box planting with this display of cacti. The pantile roof and warm-colored wall make a fitting backdrop to a mini landscape of sculptural plants and craggy rocks. The variety of forms used gives drama to the planting scheme, the tallest specimens being placed just off-center of the box.

CONTAINER

The box was made from ½ in. (12mm) marine plywood and painted with a wood preservative (see page 125 for construction details). The

front of the box was painted with cream emulsion. While the paint was still wet, red sand was scattered over the box to add some darker patches of color and texture. The interior of the box was lined with plastic, and the cacti were planted in a plastic trough, Drainage holes were punched into both layers.

PLANTS AND PLANTING

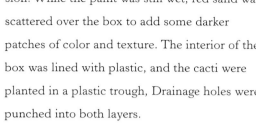

1 *Austrocephalocereus dybowskii* A columnar desert cactus that is covered in small, white, hairy spines.

2 *Cleisteocactus strausii* A tall, fast-growing columnar cactus covered with silver hairs. Well-established plants bear red flowers.

3 *Euphorbia anophila* This multistemmed, deep-green succulent is notable for its very long, dark spines.

4 *Ferocactus glaucescens* The unusual steely blue color of this cactus is decorated with prominent, creamy white spines.

5 *Ferocactus haematacanthus* This large,

round cactus forms a focal point in the box.

6 *Mammillaria wildii* This cluster desert cactus has a strong outline, its bulbous shapes hanging over the sides of the box.

7 *Opuntia leucotricha* A member of the prickly pear group of cacti. The specimen used in this box has reached its maximum size.

8 *Opuntia subulata* 'Cristata' A low-growing cactus with an attractive wavy pattern to its growth and small groups of white hairs.

CARE AND MAINTENANCE

Use a special cactus-growing mix to fill this box; it has a high content of sand and sharp grit to ensure good drainage.

The plants in this planting scheme will be happy outside in a hot, sunny spot, but in changeable climates take the box indoors during spells of cool, damp weather. Few cacti will not stand frost, but many species do need a relatively cool, dry winter period in order for them to flower well. In areas subject to frost keep them in a cool, light room indoors over the winter. Alternatively, the containers look equally effective placed on the inside of the window or in a conservatory—ideal spots when the weather is not suitable outside. Water carefully—too much water will rot the roots and stems of the plants very quickly. At the same time, it is a myth that cacti need no water at all.

SAFETY RULES
All euphorbias should be handled carefully because they exude a milky latex when damaged, and this can be irritating to the skin and harmful to the eyes.

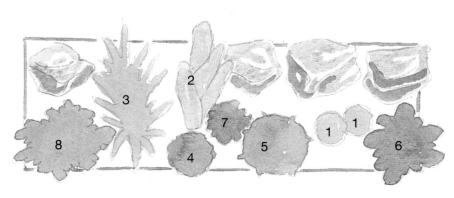

mediterranean sun

This beautiful combination of dry habitat plants evokes memories of hot Greek hillsides, and brushing a hand lightly against the foliage will release some wonderful aromas, particularly when the sun is shining on the plants. They all thrive in sun, and have either silvery gray foliage or small, leathery leaves that cut down water loss to equip them to cope with hot, dry conditions. The beauty of this planting scheme is in the subtle range of soft gray-greens of the leaves and the rich tapestry of textures they make.

CONTAINER

The same plywood box as for the cactus garden was used, but the front panel was marbled with gray paint to blend with the silvery foliage.

PLANTS AND PLANTING

1 *Brachyglottis* 'Sunshine Improved' An excellent, easy-to-grow shrub with silvery gray, rounded foliage on lax stems. The leaves have a distinctive white felt on their undersides that shines out among the other plants.

2 *Helichrysum italicum* (curry plant) The slender gray leaves of this plant have an unusual spicy aroma that is released in hot sun. The yellow button flowers add height to the planting scheme.

3 *Salvia officinalis* 'Tricolor' This culinary sage from southern Europe has beautifully variegated, soft-textured leaves of creamy white and greeny gray with a subtle touch of pink.

4 *Santolina chamaecyparissus* (lavender cotton) Bushy stems are clothed with silver filigree leaves. To retain the neat, bushy appearance, the rather untidy, small yellow flowers can be removed as soon as they appear.

5 *Thymus* x *citriodorus* A culinary thyme that gives off a strong lemon scent when the small, neat leaves are crushed. Variegated selections, including 'Silver King' and 'Argenteus', would fit well into this planting. Trailing varieties of

thyme are particularly useful at the front of window boxes to soften the edges.

6 *Thymus vulgaris* In summer, the common thyme is wreathed with soft lilac flowers that are very attractive to bees. The foliage is strongly aromatic. Trim the plant regularly to keep it compact and bushy.

CARE AND MAINTENANCE

All these plants like a warm, sunny position and very free-draining, not-too-rich soil. Although the plants are adapted to dry conditions, regular (but careful) watering will still be necessary to keep them growing well. Water thoroughly to moisten the potting mix right through, then let the surface dry out before watering again. Excess water will cause the roots and stems to rot: the foliage of plants grown in dryish soil conditions also tends to have a stronger scent than that of plants in moist soil. Pinch back flower stems and straggly branches frequently.

woodland box

This charming, natural planting would brighten any difficult, shady corner. The key elements are the miniature cyclamen: cheap and readily available in the fall they are at home in light shade. With their natural woodland appearance, ferns provide the perfect partners for the cyclamen, growing through the scattering of leaves and pushing through the crevices in the weathered timber.

CONTAINER

The base for this container is a simple fruit box made from very thin plywood, but with strong, solid wood corners. Lengths of rough, weathered timber were sawn or broken to the length of the box and nailed around it to strengthen it (see page 126 for construction details).

PLANTS AND PLANTING

The box was lined with plastic (punctured at the bottom in several places) and the base filled with 1 to 2 in. (2.5 to 5cm) of drainage material. It was then filled to within 2 in. (5cm) of the top

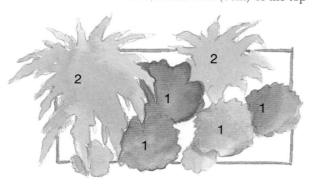

with a mixture of soilless potting mix, leafmold, and sandy grit to allow free drainage. Once planting is complete, cover the soil surface with crisp, dry oak and beech leaves.

1 *Cyclamen* Miniature cyclamen are available from most garden centers for use as house plants; although they will not stand frosts, they make good short-term outdoor subjects for this type of container. Alternatively you can buy tubers of hardy outdoor species such as *C. hederifolium* and *C. coum*, establishing these in pots that can be plunged into the box as the plants come into bud. The flowers of these species are smaller, less showy, and usually in more muted colors than the plants shown here.

2 *Polystichum setiferum* 'Herrenhausen' This easy-to-grow fern has lovely, bright green, divided fronds with an attractive arching habit, and provides the perfect contrast to the brightly colored, shuttlecock flowers of the cyclamen. Tuck plants in between the slats of the box.

CARE AND MAINTENANCE

Water sufficiently to keep the soil mix moist at all times, but take care not to splash the tops of the cyclamen tubers, or they will rot. Place the box in semishade or dappled sunlight.

shady places

Most buildings have at least one cool, shady side that would benefit from some form of planting but which provide difficult growing conditions for the plants. While it is true that most of the commonly available container plants are best suited to sunny aspects, it is certainly possible to bring color

to these dull, difficult areas, especially by using the wonderful range of foliage plants now available. Shade cast by walls or fences is often less difficult to deal with than the shade cast by trees: a wall or fence can be painted a light color to increase the amount of reflected light.

bright conifers

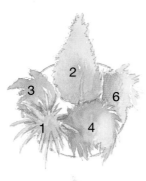

With careful watering and feeding, conifers will thrive in a container. There are plenty of conifers with colorful foliage in shades of green, blue, and gold that cope well with poor light and would certainly brighten up this shady corner.

CONTAINERS

These containers are made from concrete that has been aged to give them a suitably mellow look. Make sure this type of container has drainage holes in the base. The pots are heavy to move, especially when full, so put them in the desired position before planting.

PLANTS AND PLANTING

1 *Acorus gramineus* 'Ogon' This semiaquatic plant will have a short life in a container, but is worth growing for the contrasting shape its variegated, straplike leaf brings to the planting.

2 *Chamaecyparis lawsoniana* 'Alumigold' A conical conifer with foliage of a soft golden green shade.

3 *Chamaecyparis lawsoniana* 'Stewartii' A very popular, elegant cultivar, its foliage a rich gold in summer, becoming more of a yellow-green shade in winter.

4 *Juniperus communis* 'Green Carpet' This ground-hugging juniper is slow growing, and will trail over the side of the container, creating an elegant effect.

5 *Juniperus squamata* 'Blue Star' The stems of this slow-growing cultivar, clad in spiky leaves of a rich, deep, steel-blue color, tumble attractively over the sides of the container.

6 *Thuja orientalis* 'Collen's Gold' An outstanding slow-growing conifer with a rounded conical shape, clothed with dense vertical sprays of foliage. The tips are creamy yellow in spring, rich purple-brown in winter, and light green in summer. It keeps its color well in shady conditions.

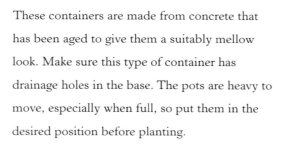
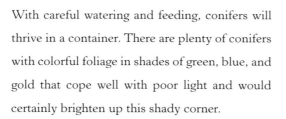

CARE AND MAINTENANCE

These conifers are not miniature varieties and will eventually outgrow their containers. However, with regular watering and feeding, they should enhance a dull spot for three or four years before they need to be transferred to the open garden. A soil-based potting mix would be best for all these plants, as it contains higher levels of nutrients than a soilless type. The acorus copes admirably with shady conditions, but must be kept very well watered at all times, or the foliage will start to turn brown.

hostas and ivy

This planting scheme exploits the varying shapes and textures of shade-loving, broad-leafed plants. A strong asymmetrical element creates an interesting balance in the design, the height of the large ivy plant giving the group more impact.

Hostas are valuable plants for providing color and form in shady areas. Their dramatic leaves occur in a range of colors, from creamy variegated cultivars, through various greens and grays, to beautiful blue-green forms with a misty bloom on the surface. The delicate flowers in muted colors make their own contribution to the planting, adding a strong vertical element. Some hostas have quite a tropical look with their opulent leaves, particularly if the plants are allowed to grow to a good size.

PLANTS AND PLANTING

1 *Hedera helix* 'Goldheart' This strongly variegated ivy adds a splash of golden color to the garden throughout the year. As winter approaches and the temperature drops, the golden mottling takes on rich pinkish tones. Ivies are vigorous climbing plants that need to be provided with sturdy supports.

2 *Hosta* There are dozens of different species and cultivars of this popular plant, all of which thrive in moist, shady conditions. The leaves have interesting textures as well as colors, many varieties having strongly furrowed or quilted leaf surfaces. Hostas often grow better in pots than in the open ground: when growing in containers they tend to be less troubled by slugs and deer.

3 *Hedera helix* 'Little Diamond' A compact evergreen ivy with diamond-shaped gray-green leaves and white variegation. It is frost hardy but needs shelter from strong winds that can cause the leaves to go brown at the edges

CARE AND MAINTENANCE

A general purpose, soilless potting mix suits these plants. The hostas die down in the fall so will need to be replaced with other subjects for winter interest. Although slugs, snails, and deer are less of a problem for plants in containers, you may still need to take some precautions against these pests, which can reduce large hosta leaves to a skeleton of veins or just stems overnight.

Provide the ivy with a support such as trellis, a tepee of branches, or canes, and tie the shoots in as they grow. Ivy does not need as frequent watering as the hostas; keep the potting mix just moist. When growing in shady conditions, the leaves of many variegated plants tend to revert to their all-green form. Look out for plain green shoots on the ivy and cut them out from the base when they appear.

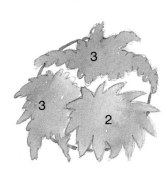

windy corner

Perhaps one of the most difficult gardening problems to cope with is a very windy location. However, most obstacles can be overcome by clever planting solutions, and some careful thought can turn disadvantages into advantages. In an exposed, windy situation, forget about using delicate plants and instead

consider introducing sculptural elements that are unaffected by weather, as exemplified by the Japanese approach to gardens. Alternatively, use plants that actually show themselves at their best when moving in the breeze.

modern grasses

As gardeners we must learn to look for those inherent qualities of plants that will help us overcome the challenges and problems of difficult growing conditions. To withstand the wind a plant must be quite flexible; in fact, movement should accentuate the beauty of the plant. To be happy and to thrive in windy conditions, a plant must be able to cope well with the very drying effect that wind has. Plants with delicate flowers and foliage are obviously ones to avoid in such situations.

Sedges and grasses are beautifully framed by this archway (right): they will look attractive here even in winter, and their sculptural lines lend them a clean, modern look.

CONTAINERS

These stylish containers are made from tin and are available in a wide range of shapes. Holes were punched in the base, which was then covered with a 2 to 3 in. (5 to 8cm) layer of gravel to provide good drainage and to help keep the containers stable in windy conditions.

PLANTS AND PLANTING

1 *Carex buchananii* The shape and overall habit of the sedge in the tall container is very grasslike. It has attractive bronze foliage and an arching shape.

2 *Festuca glauca* This beautiful tufted grass with very fine, blue-gray leaves forms a little fountain of foliage in the foreground.

3 *Stipa tenuissima* 'Ponytails' The grass in the middle container has a bold, upright habit and distinctive feathery flowering spikes that sit well above the plant.

CARE AND MAINTENANCE

Use a general purpose, soilless or soil-based potting mix. Trim off dead leaves, and give an occasional high-nitrogen liquid feed during the growing season. These plants can remain in good condition in containers for up to a year.

conifers and chimes

The wind itself becomes an integral part of this scheme, which is designed around some oriental wind chimes. The design uses a sculptural approach, combining the strong shapes of the three containers with the sturdy bamboo structure that supports the chimes. The black and brown washed color of the boxes is repeated in the bamboo. This attractive solution to a difficult gardening problem uses conifers as the backbone of the planting, as they are capable of withstanding windy conditions and give color and texture all year round.

CONTAINERS

The simple boxes are made from marine plywood painted with a black ash wood stain. Sturdy bamboo canes were painted with the same stain, then cut to size and screwed to the inner corners of the rear box. The wind chimes were tied to the bamboo with raffia. The display was finished off with gray-green pebbles that echo the color of the plants and intensify the stylized feel.

PLANTS AND PLANTING

1 *Festuca glauca* The hardy grass in the front box has a tufted habit and grows to about 12 or 16 in. (30 or 40cm) in height and spread.

The blue foliage harmonizes with the color of the conifers, and the tufted habit provides a strong textural contrast.

2 *Chamaecyparis lawsoniana* 'Columnaris Glauca' The upright conifer in the middle box has beautiful blue-green foliage and is relatively slow growing.

3 *Juniperus horizontalis* 'Bar Harbor' A prostrate, slow-growing conifer features in the rear box. Junipers in general are suitable for poor soils and harsh conditions, and are quite able to survive in difficult, windy positions.

CARE AND MAINTENANCE

Use either soil-based or soilless potting mix for this scheme. The mix should be kept just moist, so take care not to overwater the plants. In warm weather, an occasional fine mist of water over the conifer foliage will help prevent the foliage from turning brown in windy conditions.

ALTERNATIVES

There are many other slow-growing conifers that would do well in this situation. Choose from those that do not grow above 5 ft. (1.5m) in height within ten years. A good selection should be available from growers specializing in dwarf conifers and rock garden plants.

ferns for damp places

The Victorians had a passion for ferns because of their beautiful feathery leaves and ease of cultivation. To house their collections, they even created special ferneries complete with rocks to form a natural-looking environment for the plants. This has been re-created on a smaller scale in this window box—the rocks add variety of texture. Ferns will thrive in damp and shady places, making them ideal candidates for this rather difficult position on the shady side of a house.

CONTAINER

The ferns were planted in an inner plastic trough that was placed in a wooden window box. The marbled finish of the box blends with both the wall behind and the piece of stone on which it is placed. Decorative limestone rocks similar to those shown among the plants are available from most garden centers.

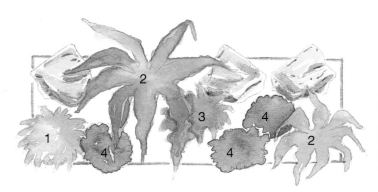

PLANTS AND PLANTING

1 *Asplenium scolopendrium* (hart's tongue fern)
There are many cultivars of the hart's tongue
fern, including several with attractively crimped
and curled edges to the leaves.

2 *Athyrium filix-femina* (lady fern) The delicate fronds of this very hardy fern are a fresh,
bright green. Again, there are many cultivars
with finely divided or crested fronds.

3 *Polystichum setiferum* (soft shield fern)
The finely divided, soft-textured fronds are
mid green. Many interesting variants of the
species can be found at specialist nurseries.

4 *Soleirolia soleirolii* (baby's tears) This mid-
green form makes a very attractive cushion of
small leaves between the ferns and rocks.

CARE AND MAINTENANCE

These ferns like a neutral to alkaline soil; they
do not grow well in acid conditions. Use a
general purpose, soilless mix, adding a handful
of ground limestone. While ferns need moisture
and require frequent watering, they do not like
to be waterlogged, and good drainage is essential if they are to thrive. After planting, mulch
the surface with leafmold or compost to help
retain moisture. If the ferns are to be a permanent planting, spread a handful of sterilized
bonemeal over the soil surface each spring, then
cover with fresh mulch.

all you need to know

window boxes and other containers

CHOOSING A WINDOW BOX

Before choosing a window box, take a good look at where it is to go—the building, plants, and box should create a pleasing and harmonious picture. Many window boxes or containers are difficult to move and once in position may need to stay there permanently, so it is important to get their position right.

Is the box to be placed in front of the window, to the side, or in between two windows? Each will give a different effect. The style of the building is also important; always choose a window box that is in keeping with the scale and period of your home. If in doubt, choose a

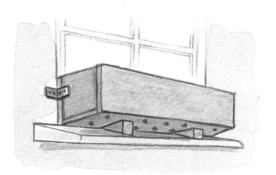

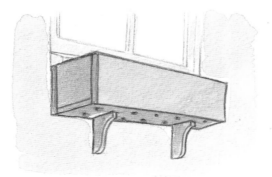

plain, simple box and allow the plants to speak for themselves.

Window boxes are made from a variety of materials, such as lead, plastic, terracotta, treated timber, and stone. Some of these may require a liner to retain moisture, and you may wish to use a plastic inner container anyway to protect the more expensive window boxes.

FIXING A WINDOW BOX

If the window opens outward, the box will have to be placed below the sill. Remember to give enough headroom to accommodate the height of the mature plants yet still allow the window to be opened. Alternatively, a box could be placed between two windows.

For sash-opening windows, or windows with top opening lights, there will often be a deep recessed sill sturdy enough take the weight of even a heavy window box. The box must still be fixed securely to the wall or window frame: this is particularly important for window boxes above the ground floor. Some sills slope down from the window and here wedges should be used to level the box. For windows without sills, or boxes that have to be positioned under the sill, use wall brackets (shown left).

BOXES WITH INNER LINERS

To get the maximum value from your boxes, use inner plastic liners. These will not only protect the containers and help retain water, but will allow you to establish a number of different planting schemes that can be placed in the window box when required, enabling you to have a succession of colorful designs that follow one another through the seasons.

If you are going to make your own window box, choose an inexpensive liner and make the outer display box to fit around it. This will allow the liner to be taken out easily when necessary. The added advantage of planting up the inner liner before it is placed in the outer box is that it avoids having to remove the window box and disturb the fixings.

WOODEN BOX CONSTRUCTION

The basic wooden troughs and window boxes used throughout this book are all made of ½ in. (12mm) marine plywood. It is only the size of the container that varies, depending on the measurements of the window and the plants to go into the box. The base, front, back, and sides are screwed together with 1 in. (2.5cm) crosshead screws. Metal, L-shaped brackets are screwed from the base to the sides (back and front) for extra support. The boxes can then be given a paint or wood stain finish to suit both the planting and the surroundings.

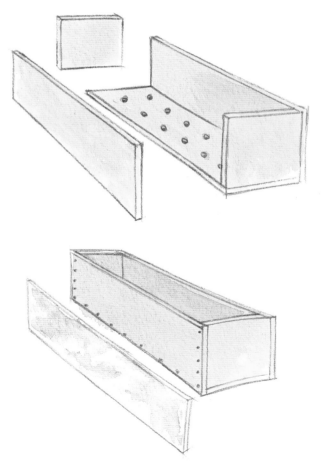

box fronts Fixing a secondary panel onto the front of the box is the simplest way of giving it a new look. The color and finish can be easily changed to go with a different style of planting.

A WEATHER BOARD BOX

A wooden window box can be given a weather board front very simply by facing it with boards of rough sawn timber or reclaimed timber from old pallets. For the vertical struts, cut seven boards to the same measurement as the height of the box (three for the front of the box and two for each end). For the front horizontal bars, cut three boards to the length of the box; for the ends of the box, cut six boards to the depth of the box, front to back (three for each end).

The vertical struts are nailed or screwed to the window box, three on the front and two on each of the sides. The horizontal boards are then nailed or screwed to the vertical struts. P.V.A. wood adhesive is used in the joints to make them stronger. Give the box a light wash of paint to coordinate with your planting scheme.

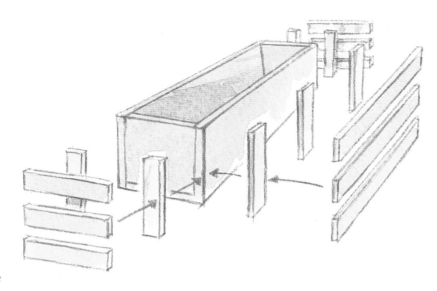

WIRE MESH AND TWIG FINISH

Use chicken wire mesh with 1 to 1¼ in. (2.5 to 3cm) diameter holes, cutting a length of mesh to fit around the box. Wrap the mesh around the box and secure it just inside the top and bottom with tacks or panel pins. Insert small twigs between the box and the mesh to give an attractive textured finish. Cut the twigs to the depth of the box when they are in position. Secure the wire mesh with extra tacks and paint the whole box with a wood stain or matte paint.

WILLOW AND CANE FENCING

Fine willow fencing is available commercially and can be cut into lengths and attached to the front of a box with panel pins. Attach the willow twigs vertically or horizontally, to create different textures.

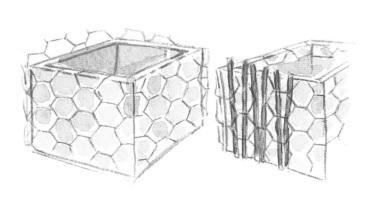

decorative finishes

There are numerous paint techniques that can be applied to wooden window boxes to vary their appearance. The finished effect will depend on the style you want to create.

MARBLING

Apply a base coat in one color to form the background for the marble effect. While this coat is still drying, very lightly brush on two other colors, covering parts of the base coat. The edges of these later coats should be feathered into the original base coat to give a misty appearance. Using a stick or stiff feather, darker colors can then be dragged over the surface at an angle to create a veined look as in marble; it helps to use a real piece of marble as a pattern while you work. When dry, protect the finished surface with clear outdoor satin or matt varnish.

STIPPLE GRANITE EFFECT

Apply a base coat of paint and allow it to dry. Use either a special stippling brush or an ordinary brush with the bristles cut down to about 1 in. (2.5cm), and dab on a range of colors to create the effect you want. (Two or three colors normally give the best result.) When dry, finish with a clear outdoor satin or matte varnish.

Sand or fine grit can be added to the paint to create a textured effect and give the box a more authentic granite appearance.

WOOD STAIN

In recent years, a selection of wood stains in a wide range of unusual colors has become available. The best effects are achieved when these are painted onto wood that has a pronounced grain. A weathered look can be achieved by sanding down the surface with sandpaper, revealing the grain underneath. Always sand in the direction of the grain, not across it.

COLOR WASHING

A weathered appearance is produced by painting the wood with a dilute solution of water-based paint. You can use any color for this, and the intensity can be varied according to the effect you want to achieve. Brush out the paint well, adding other coats to build up the color to the required strength. Rub a rag over the wet surface to work the paint into the grain, and to remove any excess.

GRAVEL, PEBBLE, AND CHIPPING FINISHES

Finishes that cover the surface of the potting mix are both decorative and practical, since they act as a mulch to help reduce moisture loss from the soil surface.

Gravel, pebbles, and chippings are available in a range of colors, sizes, and shapes, and the various types can provide a strong architectural element in a planting scheme.

DECORATING CONTAINERS WITH LEAD
Because lead is very malleable it can be used to decorate containers. Roofing lead comes in rolls and sheets and can be cut easily with pincers or strong scissors. It can be wrapped around pots, used as an edging to a box, or added as an appliqué finish to a box front. Remember to wear gloves when working with lead and to wash your hands afterward.

hanging baskets

The appearance of a hanging basket will depend on a number of factors: the materials from which it is made, how it is lined, and where it is displayed.

TYPES OF HANGING BASKET

The traditional hanging basket is made from wire twisted to create a bowl-shaped mesh. It must be strong enough to take the weight of plants and soil mixtures, which can be considerable, particularly just after they have been watered. In recent years, plastic baskets in a variety of shapes and sizes have also become readily available and are now very popular.

New and different materials such as woven willow, grass, and date palm stems are also used to create baskets of unusual design, such as inverted pyramids, cones, and cornucopias. They will last two or three seasons only, but are attractive and reasonably priced.

LINING A HANGING BASKET

Standard, twisted wire hanging baskets need a lining to keep the plants and soil in place. The customary (though somewhat old-fashioned) material used for lining baskets is sphagnum moss, and many gardeners still use this method, as they prefer its traditional appearance. To help retain moisture the moss should be lined with plastic before soilless or multipurpose potting mix is added to fill the basket.

However, moss is not always readily available from garden centers, especially in large towns and cities, and various new types of lining material have been developed. Liners made from foam rubber, coconut fiber, pressed and molded paper, and a number of other materials are now available. Some liners are intended to be used once only, but others can, with care, be used for several seasons.

The style of the liner varies according to the material from which it is made, but some are constructed with overlapping flaps that enable them to be cut to fit a range of basket sizes. These have the additional advantage of allowing the insertion of plants through the slits, thus making it easier to hide the base of the basket and achieve the traditional "all-round" effect. Other forms of liner, such as the pressed-paper types, are solid, so that it is not possible to plant through them. However, the wide selection of strong-growing trailing plants available means that this is not such a problem; they soon grow and trail sufficiently to disguise the base of the basket. One advantage of a solid basket or liner is that water retention is greatly increased, so that the potting mix does not dry out so quickly.

Baskets made from natural materials such as woven willow will need plastic liners, not only to help reduce water loss but also to prevent the discoloration that occurs if these baskets get too wet.

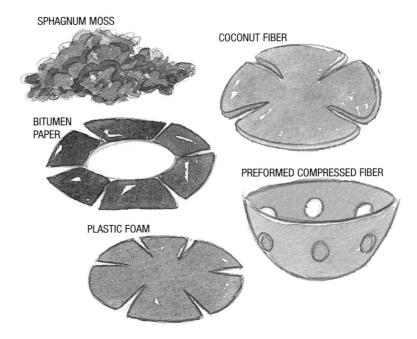

SPHAGNUM MOSS
COCONUT FIBER
BITUMEN PAPER
PREFORMED COMPRESSED FIBER
PLASTIC FOAM

PLANTING THE BASKET

Baskets with a round base can be supported in a large pot to make them easier to plant. Once the chosen liner is in place, place a layer of potting mix in the bottom of the basket. If it is possible to plant through the sides of the basket, put some trailing plants in position, inserting the roots of the plants carefully through the mesh from the outside. This is often easier to do if the young plants have some of the soil gently washed off their roots. The rootball can then be wrapped in a small cone of newspaper to enable the plants to be inserted without damage. Water thoroughly once planting is complete.

CHOOSING A SITE

For the maximum production of flowers throughout the season, choose a bright position that receives sunshine for a good part of the day. Beware of walls that are exposed to direct, full sun throughout the whole day—baskets in such a site will dry out very quickly. Light shade is acceptable, but deeper shade can be a problem unless shade-loving plants are selected.

CHOOSING A BRACKET OR HOOK

Choosing the right bracket is important—it will have to cope with a heavy load, particularly when the basket is watered. The strongest brackets are those made from wrought iron. All brackets must be secured to the wall properly, with appropriate screws and plugs.

BASKET AND BRACKET SIZES

Basket diameter	Bracket size
10 in. (25cm)	9 in. (23cm)
12 in. (30cm)	9 in. (23cm)
14 in. (35.5cm)	9 in. (23cm)
16 in. (40.5cm)	12 in. (30cm)
18 in. (46cm)	12 in. (30cm)
20 in. (51cm)	14 in. (35.5cm)
24 in. (61cm)	16 in. (40.5cm)
30 in. (76cm)	18 in. (46cm)

Choose a bracket that is long enough to accommodate the fully established basket, so that it will not knock against the wall and crush the plants. The arm must extend from the wall at least half the diameter of the basket, plus about 4 to 6 in. (10 to 15cm) for mature plants.

FIXING THE BRACKET

There are several practical factors to consider before you start drilling the holes to take the bracket. The basket should be hung at a height where it looks its best—this is not necessarily when viewed from underneath. Ease of watering must also to be taken into account—a rise and fall pulley attached to the bracket can help here. Check that once the basket is hung by its chains it will not be in the way of people passing by or passing underneath. The bracket must be secured to a reasonably smooth, level surface. Once you have chosen the final position, drill the holes and insert wall anchors. Put the bracket in place and screw the top screw in lightly; position the bottom screw and then tighten both screws as necessary.

ESTABLISHING PLANTS

Allow baskets to establish themselves for two or three weeks after planting before hanging them in their final position, to enable plant roots to settle in properly.

RISE AND FALL BRACKET

SIMPLE WOODEN BRACKET

CAST METAL BRACKET

buying plants

Always look for vigorous, healthy plants with no visible signs of pests or diseases. Select sturdy plants that are well branched at the base so they will bush out as they develop. Resist plants in full flower; although these are attractive to the eye they will already have reached their peak at the time of purchase and will not last as long after planting. Often it is cheaper—and more fun—to buy small rooted cuttings and young plants and grow them on to be planted later.

propagation

Though it is quick and easy to buy ready-grown plants from a garden center, it is very satisfying to produce plants from your own labors. Most methods of propagation are quite easy as long as you have the right facilities and are able to look after the young plants until they are ready to be planted out in a container. Most plants suitable for containers, hanging baskets, and window boxes can be propagated by seed, cuttings, or division.

SEED

Garden centers, large supermarkets, and some other stores usually have a good selection of seeds during the winter and early spring. If you are interested in trying slightly more unusual seeds, or want a specific strain or color rather than a mixture, send for catalogs from some of the specialist mail-order seed merchants.

Most seed packets come with clear instructions for sowing and growing on. The majority of seeds do best in a greenhouse, but you can get good results using a warm, well-lit window sill, preferably in a conservatory or kitchen where the temperature is kept constant.

Annuals are best sown early in the growing season for planting out after the last frosts, whereas biennials or perennials can be sown a little later in the spring. Fill a seed tray or 3 in. (8cm) pot with a commercial seed sowing mix, leveling the surface about 1 in. (2.5cm) below the rim. Water the container and let it drain thoroughly, then sprinkle the seeds over the surface. Most seed should be covered with a fine layer of sowing mix, with the exception of very fine seed.

Cover the seed container with a plastic bag or plastic propagator top and place in a greenhouse or warm position where the soil can be kept at a temperature of around 60 to 65°F (15 to 18°C). Seedlings usually appear between two and six weeks later.

CUTTINGS

A number of container plants can be grown from cuttings, including fuchsias, pelargoniums, penstemons, Surfinia petunias, and a wide range of what are now termed "patio plants." Many plants will benefit from being dipped into rooting hormone powder, which is readily available from garden centers, before being planted in the seed sowing mix.

SOFTWOOD CUTTING

Softwood cuttings are taken from nonflowering shoots in the spring and early summer. Take healthy shoots about 2 to 3 in. (5 to 7cm) in length, and cut them cleanly just below a node (where the leaf joins the stem). Remove the lower leaves and push the cutting into moistened seed sowing mix up to the first set of remaining leaves, firming it in with your fingers. Cover the pot with a clear plastic bag, and place on a warm window sill or in a greenhouse out of direct sunlight until rooted.

SEMI RIPE CUTTING

Semi ripe cuttings are good for propagating shrubby plants such as lavenders, brachyglottis, or box. Take them later in the summer, when the shoots from the early part of the year have had time to develop and become firm at the base. A propagating frame gives the best results.

Many shrubs root better if they have a little strip of the parent stem attached, called a "heel cutting." Just tear the shoot from the stem and a small heel of bark will come with it.

Fill a pot with seed sowing mix to about 1 in. (2.5cm) from the rim; a 4 in. (10cm) pot will take five or six cuttings. Insert the cutting up to about one-third of its length, firm in, water well and cover with a clear plastic bag or propagator top to keep the atmosphere moist. Place in a warm, light position out of direct sun.

Hardwood cuttings should be taken later in the year, during the dormant season. They are made from vigorous stems that have completed their first year of growth and have become woody.

Cut the stem close to its base then trim to 10 to 12 in. (25 to 30cm). Make the cut just below a bud at the bottom end and just above a bud at the top. Dig a narrow trench and fill with sharp sand. Place the cutting in the trench, burying it to about half of its length. In the spring shoots will appear, and the cutting will be ready for transplanting the following fall.

HARDWOOD CUTTING

DIVISION

Many perennial herbaceous plants can be increased by division, one of the simplest forms of propagation. This is a good way of increasing stocks of plants such as hostas, perennial lobelias, and many more.

Division is best carried out in the dormant period. It is usually done in the fall, but it can be delayed till early spring when the plants are just breaking dormancy.

The plant to be divided is lifted with roots and growth buds and is pulled or cut apart.

DIVIDING BY HAND

The method of division varies, depending on the type of plant and what sort of rootstock it has. Small, fibrous rooted plants can be divided by hand while large clumps may need to be prized apart using two forks back to back for leverage.

DIVIDING A RHIZOME

Particularly tough plants can be cut into sections with a knife. Rhizomatous plants, such as bearded iris, are divided by separating pieces off the main rootstock, each with at least one growing bud.

GENERAL CARE AND MAINTENANCE OF PLANTS

Like all plants, those in containers need to be kept in peak condition for the best results. Choose healthy plants to begin with, and use fresh, sterile potting mix each time you plant up your container. Water regularly, particularly in dry weather; in hot, sunny conditions watering may be necessary twice a day to keep the potting mix moist. Use a watering can with a long spout so that you can water through the plants and onto the soil rather than watering overhead, which can break soft shoots and damage flowerheads and buds.

Most plants benefit from weekly feeding with a liquid fertilizer—either a high-potash type, which encourages good flowering, or a balanced formula, which contains all the major nutrients required for healthy growth.

If there is an unexpected cold snap after planted-up containers have been put outside, they can be protected by covering them with gardening fabric—a very lightweight, fine, sheet-like gauze, that can be draped over plants and anchored down. It will keep out a few degrees of frost, and protect young plants and shoots.

Regular deadheading is essential to keep plants looking good and to encourage an extended flowering period. Removing dead flowerheads and leaves also helps avoid the possibility of fungal diseases taking hold.

pests and diseases

This section outlines some of the more common pests and diseases that can affect plants in window boxes and containers. If plants are kept vigorous and healthy and checked regularly, the likelihood of pests and diseases taking hold is greatly reduced. Early detection of a problem can mean that you may be able to treat it very easily, by picking off affected leaves or washing the plants with soapy water. If you do need to resort to chemical help in controlling the problem, select an appropriate remedy and follow the manufacturer's guidelines. Organic or plant-based products can provide some of the safest solutions.

PESTS

	SYMPTOMS	TREATMENT
APHIDS (BLACKFLY, GREENFLY)	Colonies of small, pale green, black or brown, soft-bodied insects can be seen on the underside of the leaves, or on young stems and buds. Sticky honeydew deposits are another indication; black sooty mold can develop on these deposits.	Wash the aphids off with soapy water or spray with an appropriate insecticide. Reduce the use of high-nitrogen liquid feeds, which encourage the soft young growth that aphids like.
WHITEFLY	Tiny, white, mothlike insects rise up from the plants in clouds whenever they are touched. Like aphids, they are sap feeders, and weaken the plants.	Whitefly are often difficult to control, as various stages of their life cycle are immune to insecticides. A suitable chemical control needs to be used several times to catch all the susceptible stages. A biological control, using a parasite called *Encarsia formosa*, is often the most successful way to deal with this pest, but it is most suitable for use in greenhouses or conservatories.
SPITTLEBUGS (FROGHOPPERS)	Frothy white foam around stems protects colonies of pale green spittlebugs. These sap feeders will destroy young shoots and are prevalent in early summer. Plants commonly affected include lavender, chrysanthemums, roses, and perennial asters.	Squash insects by hand and gently hose down affected plants.
LEAF MINER	White or brown winding tunnels are seen on leaves. These are produced by the larvae of various moths and flies. Marigolds, colombines, and chrysanthemums are particularly susceptible.	Pick off and destroy affected leaves.
RED SPIDER MITES	A silvery or yellow speckled discoloration of the leaf surface and a fine silky webbing on the underside of leaves and at the tips of shoots. The sapsucking mites themselves are minute, only just visible to the naked eye, and are a red or orange-brown color. They are prevalent in hot, dry conditions.	Spray plants with a mist of plain water regularly, especially under leaves, to increase humidity. Various chemical sprays can be used, or a biological control is available—a predator called *Phytoseiulus persimilis*. Like the biological control for whitefly, it is only really suitable for indoor use.

| SLUGS AND SNAILS | Irregular holes and tunnels eaten into bulbs, corms, tubers, leaves, and young shoots. A telltale slime trail is left behind. Many plants can be badly affected, especially those with soft, succulent, young shoots and stems. Hostas are a particular favorite. | Go out at night with a flashlight to pick off individual slugs or snails, or use traps such as saucers of beer or overturned grapefruit skins. Slug pellets are available but should be used with care to avoid affecting children, pets, and wildlife. Keep the garden tidy to reduce hiding places; lift containers off the ground and mulch the soil surface with a gravel or similar sharp material to discourage movement of the pests. |
| VINE WEEVILS | Small, fat, legless grubs about ½ in. (12mm) in length can be found in the soil or potting mix and will eat roots, tubers, and corms. The first visible symptom is usually sudden wilting of otherwise healthy plants. Vine weevils can affect plants all year round but are worst in the spring; they are a particular problem in greenhouses. | Remove and destroy any grubs found when the window box is being planted or individual plants are being prepared for planting. Commercial insecticides are available for watering or mixing into the compost. For a biological control, spray with a liquid solution containing nematodes in late spring or summer when the soil is warm. |

DISEASES

BOTRYTIS (GRAY MOLD)	A gray velvety mold on leaves, stems, and flowers during the growing season. It can affect all types of plants and is prevalent in cool, damp conditions. It usually starts on dead plant tissue but soon spreads to healthy parts.	Remove and burn affected parts of the plant and use an appropriate fungicide. Help prevent gray mold by regular deadheading, and by clearing away dead and dying leaves and flowers.
LEAF SPOTS	A range of diseases, usually seen as more or less round spots on foliage. The spots can occur in a variety of colors.	Remove affected parts and spray plants with an appropriate fungicide. Keep plants healthy, with regular feeding, to ward off an attack.
POWDERY MILDEW	A white, powdery fungus found on leaves, especially late in the season. It is encouraged by dry conditions at the roots. Mildew can affect a range of plants, with asters and sweet peas being particularly prone.	Avoid causing stress to the plants; water regularly. When seen, pick off the affected parts of the plant immediately and spray with an appropriate fungicide.
RUSTS	Raised brown, orange, white, or yellow spots on the undersides of leaves. There are several types of rust affecting a range of plants. Rust is particularly common on snapdragons, chrysanthemums, and pelargoniums.	Remove and destroy affected parts or, if badly affected, the whole plant. Spray surrounding plants with an appropriate fungicide.
VIRUS	A wide range of viruses can affect plants. Symptoms vary, but usually include weak and distorted growth with leaf discoloration.	There is no cure for viruses, so remove and destroy affected plants. Many viruses are spread by aphids, so controlling these pests will help prevent virus outbreaks.
TULIP FIRE	When tulip shoots appear they are distorted and stunted; leaves may be spotted and flowerbuds fail to open. The bulbs can show black fungal spots. This disease spreads very rapidly to neighboring plants.	Destroy affected plants and potting mix; start with fresh potting mix each year. Inspect bulbs for black spots when planting and discard any found. Dip bulbs in fungicide solution before planting to help prevent outbreaks.

plant directory

Acorus gramineus 'Ogon' (miniature variegated flag)
This grasslike plant is in fact a marginal. The variegated, straplike leaf up to 12 in. (30cm) in height provides a distinctive outline.
How to grow: Needs constantly moist soil and regular feeding. Copes well with shade.

Allium fistulosum (Welsh onion)
A clump-forming, small onion with a good flavor similar to that of scallions.
How to grow: Needs well-drained soil and plenty of sun. Clumps can be split in the spring.

Allium schoenoprasum (chives)
A relative of the onion with cylindrical leaves. Has purple-pink, drumhead flowers in early summer.
How to grow: Thrives in most soils in sun or light shade. Lime tolerant.

Allium tuberosum (garlic chive, Chinese chive)
Clump of slender, garlic-flavored leaves 10 to 12 in. (25 to 30cm) tall. Has pretty white flowers in summer.
How to grow: Well-drained, fertile soil. Propagate by division. Cut leaves down to stimulate new growth.

Anemone blanda (windflower)
Little woodland anemone with flowers in bright blue, white, or pink.
How to grow: Plant the rhizomes in groups in the fall for spring flowering. Likes moisture-retentive but well-drained soil and light shade. Soak overnight before planting.

Anethum graveolens (dill)
A culinary herb with attractive, feathery foliage that has a strong anise aroma.
How to grow: Can be grown from seed sown in spring, or bought as young plants from the garden center. Plant in a free-draining potting mix and place in full sun or light shade.

Antirrhinum 'Avalanche' (snapdragon)
A relatively new patio and container plant with unusual silvery gray foliage and creamy white flowers flecked with a touch of pink.
How to grow: Buy rooted cuttings or larger plants in spring. Position in sun or light shade all risk of frost has passed.

Aquilegia vulgaris (columbine)
This a cottage garden plant has gray-green, lobed leaves topped by slender flower stalks with nodding, spurred flowers. A number of dwarf cultivars and seed mixtures are suitable for container growing.
How to grow: Young potted plants are available from garden centers in spring. Seed sown in late spring will flower in summer the following year. Plant in moisture-retentive potting mix in an open, sunny position.

Argyranthemum frutescens (marguerite daisy)
A branching, woody-stemmed, tender perennial with light gray-green foliage, finely cut in some varieties, and daisy flowers 1 to 1½ in. (3 to 4cm) across. Flowers may be white, pale pink, or yellow; single or double.
How to grow: Likes free-draining potting mix and a sheltered position. Pinch off the tips of the shoots to promote branching. Overwinter in a frost-free place and it will provide softwood cuttings the following spring.

Artemesium absinthum
This short-lived herbaceous plant is mainly grown for its silvery gray aromatic foliage.
How to grow: Plant in well-drained but moisture-retentive potting mix.Cut back longer shoots to promote bushy growth.

Asplenium scolopendrium (hart's tongue fern)
A very hardy evergreen fern with many cultivars available, all suitable for container growing. Also sold as *Phyllitis scolopendrium*.
How to grow: Found naturally on limestone soils, but will thrive in most well-drained but moisture-retentive soils. Grows well in shade.

Aster novi-belgii (New York aster)
Dwarf asters with double or semidouble, daisy flowers in a range of pink and purple shades through late summer and the fall.
How to grow: Buy plants as the buds are starting to show color but before they are fully open. Place in a sunny position, and keep the potting mix moist but not waterlogged. Michaelmas daisies are very prone to powdery mildew; spraying with a preventive fungicide is often a good idea.

Athyrium filix-femina (lady fern)
A hardy, deciduous fern with dainty, bright green fronds; has many decorative cultivars.
How to grow: Likes humus-rich potting mix, moisture retentive but free draining. Grows best in light shade in a cool position. Easily propagated by division.

Austrocephalocereus dybowskii
A columnar desert cactus covered in small, white, hairy spines.
How to grow: Grows in the spring and summer, so pot up and increase the water in the late winter and early spring. Use specialist cactus and succulent growing mix.

Begonia semperflorens (wax begonia)
A free-flowering plant with flowers in many shades of pink, salmon, and red as well as white. Leaf color can vary from bright green to dark bronze.
How to grow: This half-hardy plant is best treated as an annual; buy after the last frosts. Look for sturdy plants with plenty of basal shoots, and plant in fertile, well-drained potting mix in full sun or light shade.

Begonia tuberhybrida
A trailing begonia well suited to hanging baskets; the double and semidouble flowers hang down in large clusters and look best when viewed from below. There are many good strains in a wide range of colors.
How to grow: Buy sturdy young plants with several sideshoots. Half hardy, so set out after the last frosts. Use free-draining potting mix and keep it just moist at all times. Liquid feed regularly for good flowering.

Beta vulgaris 'Rainbow Mixed' (chard)
A delightful ornamental vegetable that has leaf stems of orange, yellow, or white. Ruby

chard has bright red stems.
How to grow: Seed is freely available. Keep the plants well watered. Young leaves are excellent to add color to salads.

Brachycome (Swan River daisy)
A half-hardy plant with beautiful, starlike, daisy flowers in white, yellow, or blue, set in a fine tracery of feathery, mid-green foliage.
How to grow: Use general purpose, fertile potting mix and give regular liquid feeds during the flowering season. Pinch off the shoot tips to encourage branching. The plants tolerate light shade, but full sun is best.

Brachyglottis 'Sunshine Improved'
A shrub with gray foliage and white felt on the underside of leaves. Previously known as *Senecio greyii*.
How to grow: Easy to grow and will tolerate poor soil; good for dry sites. It needs well-drained potting mix and an open, sunny position. The yellow, daisy flowers can be removed if they make the plant look untidy.

Brassica oleracea (ornamental cabbage)
Excellent for bringing color into winter planting schemes, these plants come in a range of shades. They are very hardy, and falling temperatures intensify their colors.
How to grow: Choose compact plants without any yellowing outside leaves. Buy in the fall to provide winter color, and in the early spring for spring and early summer. Easy to grow in any good potting mix.

Buxus sempervirens 'Suffruticosa' (dwarf box)
A versatile evergreen foliage plant, box is very hardy and frost resistant. As the temperature drops the small, neat, green leaves take on gold and orange hues
How to grow: Plants will tolerate most soils and grow well in general purpose potting mix. When grown in containers, give the roots protection during cold winters, by wrapping insulating material (such as bubble wrap) round the pots.

Calibrachoa (million bells)
An excellent summer trailing plant wreathed with flowers in many shades of pink, lilac, and soft golden yellow.
How to grow: These plants can be over-wintered and grown from cuttings or bought from garden centers. They are frost tender and thrive in free-draining potting mix. Feed regularly throughout the season with balanced liquid fertilizer.

Campanula medium (Canterbury bells)
A lovely, delicate blue, white, or pink campanula with "cup-and-saucer" flowers. Choose one of the dwarf varieties such as 'Chelsea Pink' to grow in containers.
How to grow: Usually a biennial, but some of the dwarf types will flower in as little as 12 weeks from a spring sowing. Buy pot-grown plants just as the buds are starting to open. These plants like a sunny site and free-draining potting mix.

Campanula rotundifolia (harebell)
With delicate blue flowers, this biennial is rarely found in pots but seed is available.
How to grow: Sow seed in spring to flower the following year, and grow the plants in small pots that can be plunged into the outer container. The flowers are soon over, so replace the plants quickly. Harebells like well-drained soil and a sunny aspect.

Carex buchananii (bronze sedge)
A sedge with a grasslike habit and bronze foliage. It survives well in containers.
How to grow: Keep the potting mix moist throughout the growing season.

Celeisteocactus strausii
A columnar desert cactus, clump-forming and covered in white hairs.
How to grow: Growing period is spring and summer so pot up in late winter or early spring and increase the water regime. Large specimens will produce red flowers.

Centranthus ruber (valerian)
A short-lived perennial with heads of small, star-shaped, reddish pink flowers above rather fleshy leaves.
How to grow: Use general purpose potting mix with a little lime added. This plant soon becomes leggy in containers, when it is best discarded. Plants are available in pots from garden centers, but they self-seed very readily, and seedlings can be potted up.

Chamaecyparis lawsoniana (Lawson cypress)
A relatively slow-growing conifer available in a vast range of varieties, several of which are suitable for containers. 'Alumigold' has yellow-green foliage, while 'Stewartii' has foliage that is more gold than yellow, becoming greener in the winter. 'Columnaris Glauca' is one of the best Lawson cypresses, forming a narrow column of a beautiful blue-green color. It is not a miniature but with correct watering and feeding will be fine in a container for a number of years.
How to grow: Look for healthy plants well clothed with foliage down to the base. Make sure they have adequate moisture at the roots and protect the plants from drying winds. If trimming is necessary, do not cut back into the old wood, as it will not regrow.

Chrysanthemum (pot mum)
These plants, in a wide range of colors, are available in flower year round. Recently, larger, dome-shaped, multiflowered plants, which have been grown outdoors to flower in their natural season of late summer and fall, have become very popular.
How to grow: Use fertile, free-draining potting mix and keep the plants well watered. Buy sturdy, well-branched plants in bud.

Cleistocactus strausii (silver torch)
A tall, columnar cactus covered with silver spines. Relatively fast growing, it adds a powerful vertical dimension to a planting of succulents and cacti.
How to grow: Use special cacti and succulent potting mix, and water carefully. Let the surface of the soil dry out between waterings. Set in a hot, sunny position, and move indoors well before the first frosts.

Clematis Petit Faucon ('Evisix')
This nonclinging variety has blooms of deep indigo blue with yellow anthers that flower from mid summer to the fall. A deciduous plant, mature height of about 3½ ft. (1m).
How to grow: Likes moisture-retentive soil with its roots in cool shade.

Cotoneaster species
A large family of shrubs with varied habits from creeping, prostrate plants to large, upright bushes: use dwarf cultivars for

containers. All have flowers in early summer and most have orange, yellow, or red berries in the fall and winter.
How to grow: Buy small shrubs in pots, plant in free-draining but moisture-retentive soil. Keep well watered.

Crocosmia 'Lucifer'
A striking, sculptural plant around 5 ft. (1.5m) tall, with bold, straplike leaves and wands of flame-red flowers.
How to grow: Plant corms in the fall or spring, or buy pot-grown plants as they come into flower. Requires well-drained soil and a sunny position. Easy to increase by division.

Crocus sieberi (crocus)
One of the earliest of the spring-flowering bulbs and corms, there are many varieties available in a range of colors and flower sizes.
How to grow: Buy corms in the fall for planting in containers, or buy as potted bulbs in the spring. Plant in free-draining potting mix and place in a sunny position as they come into flower.

Cuphea llavea 'Tiny Mice'
A slightly trailing, spreading plant with pointed, mid-green foliage and a red and blue flower that looks rather like a mouse's face close to—hence the name. Free flowering over a long period.
How to grow: A tender perennial that needs well-drained potting mix but should not be allowed to dry out. Available as small plants in spring.

Cyclamen persicum (florist's cyclamen)
A winter-flowering pot plant with rounded, marbled leaves and distinctive shuttlecock flowers in a range of colors. Large or minia-ture varieties are available.
How to grow: These pot plants are marketed for indoor use, but they like cool conditions and will grow outdoors for a short while in a sheltered, frost-free position. Use them to add temporary color to boxes. Choose sturdy plants with plenty of buds, and take care not to splash water on top of the tuber.

Echeveria species
Attractive, tender succulents with a strong rosette shape and concentric swirls of broad,

fleshy, gray-green or blue-green foliage, depending on the species and variety.
How to grow: Likes full sun and well-drained soil. Plants are not frost hardy and must be overwintered under cover in cold areas.

Erica species (heather)
Small, hardy, shrubby plants with needlelike foliage and spires of flowers in late summer and early fall. There are many cultivars, with flowers in shades of purple, pink, white, and red; some also have attractive colored foliage, especially in winter.
How to grow: Most heathers prefer lime-free soil (though *Erica carnea* is more lime tolerant) so use acid potting mix. Place in full sun and keep just moist.

Erysimum cheiri (wallflower)
Fragrant spring flowers in a range of colors. Seed of several strains is available, in mixed or single colors.
How to grow: This biennial is sometimes available in the fall as bare-root plants for potting on, or can be grown from seed sown in mid summer. More-established young plants may be found in the spring for early summer flowering. Grow in well-drained potting mix with a little lime added.

Erythronium revolutum (trout lily)
A lovely spring-flowering plant with mottled foliage and pink flowers with reflexed petals.
How to grow: Plant bulbs in the fall or buy potted plants in spring. Grow in moisture-retentive potting mix in a shady spot.

Euphorbia species
A huge genus of plants, many of which are succulents that are relatively easy to grow.
How to grow: Place outside during the summer months. Use very free-draining potting mix and water sparingly, increasing the watering in late spring and summer. All euphorbias should be handled carefully because when damaged they exude a milky latex that can be irritating to the skin and harmful to the eyes.

Ferocactus species (barrel cactus)
Species used in the book include the globular *F. haematacanthus* and *F. glaucescens*, which has creamy white spines and an unusual

steely blue color. These slow-growing cacti form a spherical or elongated barrel shape, and are covered with prominent red or yellow spines. There are several species.
How to grow: Use free-draining cacti and succulent potting mix. Let the surface of the compost dry out between waterings, and grow in a sheltered position in full sun. Move under cover in late summer.

Festuca glauca (blue fescue)
A beautiful tufted grass with fine, blue-gray leaves springing from the center.
How to grow: Happy in any general purpose potting mix in a sunny site. Easy to multiply by division of the clumps in spring.

Fragaria x *ananassa* (strawberry)
A well-known fruiting plant ideal for containers, with attractive scallop-edged leaves and white flowers, followed by the bright red fruits. Many varieties are available for fruiting at different seasons. Small-growing alpine types are good for small areas.
How to grow: Buy young, container-grown plants in spring and early summer. Plant in general purpose potting mix and place in full sun or light shade. Keep the roots moist and liquid feed regularly.

Francoa sonchifolia (bridal wreath)
A perennial plant with deeply lobed foliage and wands of pinkish-white, long-lasting flowers in summer.
How to grow: Plant in well-drained soil in light shade to full sun.

Fritillaria
A large genus of late spring flowers found in meadows from western Asia through most of Europe. *F. acomptela* has bell-shaped flowers of deep purple edged with orange and carried on 8 to 12 in. (20 to 30cm) stems. *F. meleagris* has a check pattern on the petals.
How to grow: Meleagris will naturalize easily in moist but well-drained potting mix.

Fuchsia 'Gartenmeister bonstedt'
This bush fuchsia has tubular flowers about ¾ in. (2cm) long in a warm terracotta color and rich green foliage.
How to grow: Use general purpose soil mix and keep moist at all times. This fuchsia is

not frost hardy; keep under cover for the winter. It will produce plenty of shoots suitable for softwood cuttings in spring.

Gaultheria mucronata (pernettya)
An evergreen shrub with pointed, dark green, glossy leaves and small, white, bell-shaped flowers in early summer. On female cultivars these are followed by long-lasting fruits in bright pink, red, lilac, or white.
How to grow: These plants need lime-free (ericaceous) potting mix. Keep the roots moist, and grow in light shade. For good berry production, plant one male cultivar to pollinate three females, though plants already in berry can be bought from garden centers.

Hebe 'Autumn Glory' (shrubby veronica)
The rich purple flowers of this fall-flowering shrub bring vibrancy to any planting scheme.
How to grow: In the spring buy stocky, container-grown plants with good basal branching. In the fall, buy them just as they are coming into flower. They like free-draining soil and a sheltered position in full sun. Though moderately frost hardy, prolonged cold weather can kill this plant.

Hedera helix (ivy)
Many varieties of ivy are available, and most are easy to grow.
How to grow: Not fussy about soil or position, but full sun improves the foliage color of variegated types. Provide the plant with support for it to climb.

Helichrysum cymosum
A half-hardy plant with clusters of bright, mustard yellow, small pom-pom flowers in profusion.
How to grow: Plant in well-drained soil in full sun or light shade.

Helichrysum italicum (curry plant)
A branching shrub with slender, silvery gray leaves that have a strong, spicy smell.
How to grow: This plant will cope with most aspects, but is best in full sun or light shade in free-draining soil. Pinch off the tips of shoots to encourage bushy growth. The yellow flowers can be removed if they detract from the plant's appearance.

Helichrysum petiolare
This trailing plant usually has silver foliage, but the cultivar 'Limelight' has lime-green leaves and adds a touch of brightness to planting schemes.
How to grow: Plant out in well-drained soil after the risk of frost is over. This tender plant is best in a sunny or lightly shaded position. Take care not to overwater.

Heliotropium arborescens (heliotrope)
Heads of small, rich purple flowers are carried above wrinkled, mid-green leaves and have a very strong, sweet fragrance. A delight for summer planting.
How to grow: Raise from seed sown in spring or buy young plants in spring. Prefers rich, moisture-retentive potting mix. Place in full sun or light shade.

Hosta species
These plants have lush foliage and are ideal for shady spots. There are many cultivars of varying sizes, with superb textured, colored, and variegated leaves. Delicate spikes of bell flowers are also attractive.
How to grow: Hostas thrive in moist, shady conditions. Plant in humus-rich, moisture-retentive potting mix and keep well watered. These plants are attractive to slugs and snails; hostas in containers usually fare better, but still need protection.

Hyacinthus 'City of Haarlem' (hyacinth)
This is the most yellow of all the hyacinths, a soft primrose color, with a compact stem wreathed in flowers.
How to grow: Plant bulbs in the fall, or buy pot-grown plants in early spring, just as the buds are starting to show color. Plunge plants into the window box in their pots so that they can be removed from the display once the flowers are over. The flower spikes are heavy, and may need discreet staking.

Hydrangea macrophylla (mophead hydrangea)
A hardy shrub with large, rounded heads of florets in pink, red, lilac, or blue. Flower color depends on both cultivar, and acidity of the potting mix—acid soil gives blue flowers, limey soil gives pink or red.
How to grow: Buy sturdy, well-branched plants and set them in light shade in moisture-retentive potting mix. Proprietary fertilizers and additives can be used to intensify or alter flower color.

Ilex x *altaclerensis* 'Golden King' (variegated holly)
A female variety that does not bear berries very reliably. The lightly prickly leaves are margined with creamy yellow.
How to grow: This variety will eventually become too large for a container, but can be kept in good condition for a while by careful watering and regular feeding. Position in full sun in free-draining soil.

Impatiens walleriana (busy Lizzie)
Low-growing plants with green or bronzy leaves and masses of colorful, spurred flowers all through the summer. Many different strains are available.
How to grow: Buy young plants or plugs in the bedding plant season, during spring. Plant in general purpose potting mix and set out after the last frosts. They cope well with light shade but also enjoy full sun.

Iris danfordiae
A spring-flowering species growing from a corm, this iris has bright yellow flowers marked with green spots that are held on 2 to 4 in. (5 to 10cm) tall stiff stems. *I. reticulata* has purple-blue flowers and pointed leaves.
How to grow: Plant corms in the fall or buy potted plants in spring. Plunge into the display in their pots when they start to show color; they have a short flowering season.

Jamesbrittenia 'Indigo'
Sometimes sold as sutera or sumatra, this plant bears oval leaves on branching stems, with small, purple, yellow-eyed flowers in summer and early fall.
How to grow: Buy young plants in late spring and put out after all risk of frost has passed. Likes well-drained soil and a sunny, sheltered position.

Juniperus species (juniper)
There are many species of this conifer, some upright and others prostrate and ground hugging. They have spiky, often steely blue foliage and cope well with poor growing

conditions. Choose slow-growing varieties for container planting. *J. communis* 'Green Carpet', *J. squamata* 'Blue Star', and *J. horizontalis* 'Bar Harbor' are featured in this book, but there are many other suitable cultivars.
How to grow: Plant young specimens in general purpose potting mix in an open, sunny position; avoid overwatering. Suitable for difficult, windy situations.

Lactuca sativa (lettuce)
Lots of attractive varieties are available, including 'Lollo Rosso', a popular, curled-leaf, red-tipped cultivar. Cut-and-come-again varieties are the best for containers, as they give a continuing display.
How to grow: Easily raised from seed. Plant seedlings in rich, moisture-retentive potting mix in sun or light shade. Keep well watered.

Lantana camara
A tender, evergreen shrub with wrinkled, textured leaves and clustered heads of tubular flowers in shades of yellow, pink, orange, and red, often with several different shades within one flowerhead.
How to grow: Plant out in summer, well after all risk of frost has passed. Use general purpose, free-draining potting mix, which should be kept just moist at all times.

Lathyrus odoratus (sweet pea)
Mainly climbing plants with winged, fragrant flowers in a wide range of colors. The Spencer strain is among the best.
How to grow: Sow seeds in autumn or spring, or buy young plants in spring. Grow in moisture-retentive, rich potting mix, and water and feed regularly through the season, using a high-potash liquid fertilizer. Cut the flowers before they set seed; otherwise the flowering period will be reduced.

Laurentia axillaris (isotoma)
This plant (also called *Solenopsis*) produces domes of feathery, mid-green foliage wreathed with a myriad of starlike blue flowers with a silvery white reverse. 'Blue Star' is a popular cultivar.
How to grow: Set out young plants after all risk of frost has passed. Use free-draining potting mix.

Laurus nobilis (sweet bay)
This classic culinary bay has pointed, leathery, dark green, pungent leaves and creamy, star-shaped flowers in spring. Usually grown in containers as topiary specimens.
How to grow: Although hardy to zone 8, the foliage can be damaged by cold winds and frosts, so plant in a sheltered position and give protection in very cold weather. Use free-draining potting mix (preferably soil-based), and liquid-feed the plants regularly throughout the growing season. It is best to buy ready-trained trees the size you require.

Lavandula angustifolia (common or French lavender)
The misty gray-green stems and aromatic leaves are topped by the familiar, beautifully scented flower spikes. Many good cultivars are available: 'Hidcote', with short, stocky growth and deep lavender blue flowers, is one of the best.
How to grow: Use well-drained compost and set plants in sun or light shade. Trim back hard after flowering. Easy to propagate by semiripe cuttings in summer.

Lilium (lily)
There are many species and cultivars available, in a range of colors from pure white through pink, orange, and red to yellow, sometimes with heavily speckled petals. Those used in this book include *L. longiflorum* (Easter lily), with pure white, very fragrant flowers; 'Chinook', a short-stemmed golden lily overlaid with orange; and 'Montreaux', a pink lily with a graceful habit.
How to grow: Plant bulbs in the fall, or buy potted plants in the spring. Plunge into the display in their pots so they can be removed after flowering. Well-drained soil is essential; put some sharp sand under and around the bulbs when they are planted to improve drainage. Will grow in light shade or full sun.

Linaria 'Blue Lace' (toadflax)
A pretty trailing plant with tiny blue flowers set off against small, gray-green leaves.
How to grow: A hardy annual available from garden centers during the bedding plant season. Plant in free-draining potting mix in full sun or light shade.

Lobelia species
The most familiar lobelia for window boxes and hanging baskets is *L. erinus*, a small, mound-forming annual with mid-green leaves and usually blue, two-lipped flowers. *L.* x *speciosa*, a half-hardy perennial sometimes treated as an annual, produces tall spikes of flowers: 'Fan Scarlet' is one of the best cultivars. *L. valida* is a new introduction, with 12 in. (30cm) stems clustered with deep blue, lightly scented flowers.
How to grow: Buy young plants in the bedding plant season and plant in moisture-retentive, fertile potting mix after all risk of frost has passed. Keep moist and give regular, high-potash feeds to ensure a long-lasting display.

Lycopersicon esculentum (tomato)
Several varieties of tomato have been bred for patio growing, and are ideal for window boxes. Among suitable cultivars are 'Bonsai hybrid', 'Teardrop hybrid', and 'Jolly hybrid'.
How to grow: Raise from seed sown under cover in early spring or buy young plants from garden centers for planting out after the last frosts. Tomatoes need fertile, free-draining but moisture-retentive potting mix, and a warm, sunny position for the fruit to ripen well. Water frequently and give high-potash liquid feeds weekly. In small containers, pinch off the growing tips once two trusses of fruit have set.

Mammillaria wildii
A cluster desert cactus. Its main growing period is spring and summer.
How to grow: Increase the water regime in the late winter and early spring. Use special cactus and succulent growing mix.

Mentha villosa 'Variegata' (pineapple mint)
An attractive mint, with rounded leaves variegated cream and green, and a fruity aroma.
How to grow: Plant in moisture-retentive potting mix. Grows in light shade or full sun.

Mesembryanthemum variegatum 'Rose'
This frost-tender plant with trailing variegated leaves and dainty pink double-daisy flowers will bloom throughout the season.
How to grow: Use free-draining potting mix and feed regularly.

Monopsis 'Midnight'.
A South African trailing plant ideal to cascade from a basket or over the front of a window box. It has flowers the color and shape of violets.
How to grow: Buy as a young plant in the bedding plant season; half hardy, so do not plant out until after the last frosts. Although it likes full sun it will tolerate light shade. Water and liquid-feed regularly.

Muscari armeniacum (grape hyacinth)
A spring-flowering bulb with spires of true blue, bell-shaped flowers with a slight scent.
How to grow: Plant bulbs in the fall in pots and plunge into containers as flower spikes appear. Use general purpose potting mix; and keep just moist over the winter.

Nicotiana species (tobacco plant)
The trumpet-shaped flowers of the tobacco plant generally have a strong, sweet perfume in the evening. Several species and cultivars are available, ranging from dwarf bedding types to specimens that grow up to 5 ft. (1.5m) tall. The old-fashioned varieties tend to have a stronger scent than some colorful modern bedding strains.
How to grow: Seed can be sown in spring, or young plants bought in the bedding plant season. They like a sunny position and well-drained soil.

Ocimum minimum (bush basil)
A half-hardy herb much used in Italian cooking. It has small, oval leaves with a strong clove scent and makes a neat, rounded bush.
How to grow: Raise from seed or buy young plants in spring and plant out after all risk of frost has passed. Grow in well-drained potting mix in a warm, protected site.

Ophiopogon planiscapus 'Nigrescens' (black mondo grass)
The black, straplike leaf of this plant looks extremely good in settings that require a modern feel, or in natural settings where a contrast between texture, form, and color is required.
How to grow: This hardy, clump-forming plant will grow in sun or light shade in fertile, free-draining potting mix.

Opuntia species (prickly pear cactus)
There are many species, usually with round, flattened pads joined at angles and covered with spines. Species include *O. leucotricha* and *O. subulata* 'Cristata', which has a wavy edge to its growth.
How to grow: Grow in special cactus and succulent potting mix, and water carefully. Take the plants under cover before temperatures start to drop in the fall. The bristly spines are irritating to the skin, so take care.

Origanum vulgare 'Aureum' (golden marjoram)
A low, spreading, perennial, culinary herb with neat, oval, aromatic leaves of a bright, golden green. Has a few heads of small, pinkish white flowers in summer.
How to grow: Plant in free-draining potting mix and keep moderately watered during the growing season. Pinch off shoot tips to promote bushy growth; remove flower stems if they spoil the appearance of the plant.

Passiflora citrina (yellow passionflower)
A recently introduced climbing plant with lush leaves and delicate, soft yellow flowers. Semi-evergreen, but not frost hardy.
How to grow: Buy plants in late spring or early summer and grow in general purpose potting mix. Set out in a sheltered, sunny position after all risk of frost has passed. Provide the climbing stems with support.

Pelargonium species and varieties (geranium)
These plants are among the most popular subjects for containers. There are many cultivars derived from *P.* x *hortorum* (bedding geranium), some with attractively variegated leaves, and flowers in a range of red, pink-salmon, and white tones. Cultivars derived from *P. peltatum* (ivy-leafed geranium) have fleshy, ivy-shaped leaves on lax, tumbling stems and freely produced heads of brightly colored flowers; they are ideal for hanging baskets and the front of window boxes. Finally there are the scented-leaf varieties. These have a great range of leaf shapes, all of which are strongly aromatic, especially when handled. The scents range from citrus, through rose and pine to peppermint and pepper. 'Lady Plymouth' and 'Candy Dancer' are two varieties that were used in

this book but there are many others available from specialist growers.
How to grow: Look for stocky, well-branched young plants and set them out after the risk of frost has passed, in free-draining soil in a sunny or lightly shaded position. Feed flowering plants weekly with a high-potash liquid feed. Plants are not frost hardy, but can be overwintered to produce shoots for softwood cuttings in spring.

Penstemon cultivars
Lovely perennial plants with colorful, tubular flowers. Many different cultivars are available.
How to grow: Plant in fertile, free-draining potting mix in an open, sunny position. Plants are usually frost hardy but can be killed by cold winters. Back up stock with cuttings, which root easily if taken in the fall.

Perovskia atriplicifolia (Russian sage)
Aromatic gray foliage and gray-blue spires of flowers in late summer and early fall.
How to grow: Needs well-drained potting mix and an open, sunny position. In spring cut the old flowering stems back to about 6 in. (15cm) from the base.

Petroselinum crispum (parsley)
A biennial herb valuable for its attractive curled leaf. For culinary purposes, flat-leafed or French parsley has better flavor.
How to grow: Sow seed in early spring; it is very slow to germinate. Young plants are available from garden centers. Grow in an open, sunny position in rich, well-drained potting mix; water regularly. Two sowings a year are best for continuous picking.

Petunia
Surfinia hybrids provide an outstanding display of weather-resistant, trumpet-shaped flowers in white, pink, or purple shades. They always perform well and produce a cascade of color. *Hybrida nana compacta* 'Super cascade' have huge flowers up to 4 in. (10cm) in diameter and flower early in the season.
How to grow: Available as young rooted cuttings or as more-established potted plants in the bedding plant season. Grow in well-drained, general purpose compost in sun or light shade.

Photinia x *fraseri*
An evergreen shrub with red stems and bright red young leaves.
How to grow: Best grown in free-draining potting mix in full sun or light shade. Only moderately frost hardy; overwinter in a conservatory or sunroom.

Polystichum setiferum 'Herrenhausen' (soft shield fern)
The soft-textured fronds of this hardy fern are finely divided, and a fresh, bright green.
How to grow: Use humus-rich growing mix with a little lime, and keep moist. Thrives in light shade.

Primula species
The English primrose (strains of *P. vulgaris*) is available in pots through the winter and spring. Many strains are available, with relatively large, colorful flowers in shades of yellow, red, purple, pink, and white, held singly on slender, wiry stems. Polyanthus-type primroses (*P. elatior*) carry flowers in clusters on the top of sturdy 6 to 8 in. (15 to 20cm) stems. Both plants form a neat rosette of tongue-shaped, crinkled, light green leaves. *P. denticulata* (drumstick primrose) has distinctive round heads of purple flowers.
How to grow: Easy to care for, and will grow well in soilless potting mix in full sun or light shade. Keep moist at all times.

Pyracantha rogersiana 'Golden Charmer' (firethorn)
A spiny shrub with hawthornlike, white flowers in early summer followed by yellow berries in the fall and winter. There are also red- and orange-berried varieties.
How to grow: Buy small pot-grown plants and grow in fertile, general purpose potting mix. Use as short-term decoration in a box.

Raphanus sativus (radish)
A quick-growing salad vegetable with red or red and white edible roots that mature about six weeks from sowing. Choose a round-rooted cultivar for containers.
How to grow: Sow seed in spring and transplant seedlings into the display containers as required. Keep well watered and place in a sunny spot. Pull for eating when the roots are large enough.

Rosa cultivars (rose)
One of our best-loved flowers. Most useful for containers are the miniature or patio roses, which form compact bushes of various sizes according to variety. Many colors are available. Some of the larger roses are suitable for areas such as balconies and patios; one of the best is 'Queen Elizabeth', a soft pink floribunda with a tall, upright habit.
How to grow: Choose well-branched, container-grown plants; miniature and patio varieties are best purchased just as they are coming into bud. Plant in fertile, general purpose potting mix and place in full sun or light shade. Feed regularly with a high-potash liquid fertilizer. Deadhead frequently. Trim back minature roses after flowering for a second flush.

Salvia officinalis 'Icterina' (variegated sage)
A semi-evergreen culinary herb with pointed, wrinkled leaves that are strongly aromatic and attractively variegated. 'Tricolor' has green, gray, white, and pink in the leaves.
How to grow: Buy strong, bushy plants in spring or autumn; grow in general purpose potting mix in full sun. In areas with heavy frosts, choose a sheltered position for the plants in winter. Trim shoots regularly to prevent plants from becoming leggy.

Santolina chamaecyparissus (lavender cotton)
The aromatic silver foliage is finely cut and has a woolly texture. Small, round yellow flowers in summer, on long, rather lax stems.
How to grow: Set in a sunny position in free-draining potting mix; do not overwater. The rather untidy-looking flowers can be removed to retain the plant's neat, bushy appearance.

Scaevola aemula
A wonderful hanging basket plant with trailing stems covered with violet-blue fan-shaped flowers throughout the season.
How to grow: Buy sturdy young plants before they have produced long shoots, as this makes them easier to plant. Use well-drained potting mix and grow in sun or light shade.

Sisyrinchium striatum
This clump-forming plant provides a strong vertical form in a planting scheme, with long, narrow, upright, light green leaves and, in summer, vertical flower spikes wreathed in small, creamy yellow flowers.
How to grow: Sisyrinchium prefers moisture-retentive soil and a position in full sun, but tolerates light shade. Needs frequent watering when grown in containers.

Soleirolia soleirolii (baby's tears)
A creeping plant with tiny, round, bright green leaves that carpet the soil surface. 'Aurea' is a golden-leafed form, and 'Variegata' has a silvery variegation.
How to grow: Likes moist, but not water-logged, growing mix. The foliage is killed by frost, but the plant usually recovers in spring. It is easily propagated by division, but can become an invasive weed in the garden, so keep it restricted to containers.

Stephanandra tanakae
A hardy deciduous shrub with attractive fern-like foliage.
How to grow: Plant in light potting mix. It will sucker freely once established .

Stipa tenuissima 'Ponytails'
A feathery grass with tall, very distinctive flowering spikes that sit above the plant.
How to grow: Hardy to zone 7, this plant will tolerate harsh conditions and an exposed site. Buy strong, tufted plants in spring and early summer, and grow in well-drained, general purpose potting mix.

Sutera cordata (bacopa)
A spreading, trailing plant with small, neat, bright green leaves and numerous white or lavender flowers that is ideal for hanging baskets and the front of window boxes. There is a golden-variegated form called *Sutera* 'Olympic Gold'.
How to grow: Put this half-hardy plant outside after all risk of frost has passed. Buy fairly small plants that have not started to trail too far. They like moist but well-drained potting mix, and a sunny position.

Tagetes erecta (African marigold)
Half-hardy annuals with divided, dark green, pungent leaves and large, fully double daisy-type flowers in summer. Flowers are usually yellow and orange, but 'Vanilla' is the first white hybrid.